MILLIONAIRE
SECRETS IN YOU

Uncover, Unlock and Unleash
The Success Within You

KEVIN KLIMOWSKI
JODI NICHOLSON

STERLING PUBLISHING GROUP
WWW.STERLINGPUBLISHINGGROUP.COM

Millionaire Secrets In You

This is a work of non-fiction. This publication is designed to provide accurate information on the subject matter covered. It is sold with the understanding that the publisher is not engaged in rendering professional services or advice. The information is not intended to replace any legal council or other professional directives. If professional services or advice or other assistance is required, the services of a professional should be sought.

ISBN: 978-0-9845010-0-7

Library of Congress Control: On File With The Publisher

Published by The Sterling Publishing Group, USA
www.SterlingPublishingGroup.com

Cover Design & Layout: Jodi Nicholson | AFGOC.com
Cover Photo: Brian Sawin | BrianSawin.com

This book may be ordered by calling 813.658.5026
or by visiting: http://www.AFGOC.com

Printed in the United States of America

Motivational / Self Help

IN MEMORY

In loving memory of
Kevin Klimowski
May 15, 1964 – January 2, 2011

I have chosen to continue the journey that
Kevin and I began in 2000 ...
to honor our commitment to excellence,
to teach, learn, grow and inspire!

This book is dedicated to
the unique spirit in each of us,
may it be ignited in the passionate pursuit
of excellence and humbled
in the ultimate appreciation of success.

Jodi Nicholson

CONTENTS

CONTENTS

MILLIONAIRE
SECRETS IN YOU

Uncover, Unlock and Unleash
The Success Within You

INTRODUCTION

If you want something new in your life, you must change what you do in your life.

I believe that we all have everything inside of us to be as successful as we want to be. The thing is most people don't realize the incredible potential that lies inside of them. This book is designed to open your eyes, make you aware, and build confidence so that you can accomplish whatever it is you want in your life. This book will guide you and provide for you the foundation that makes the *"successful"* successful, and what you need to do to follow your desired path.

Although this book may seem small in size it contains the secrets of the successful people in the world. No fluff, no hype, and no stories, just proven principles that have worked and will continue to work over and over again for the people who implement and follow them.

The book has been divided into 3 sections: Mindset, Money and Action Steps To Success. The first works with the mind and is the foundation to get you thinking differently because your inner world is what determines the success in your outer world. Helen Keller puts it so eloquently, *"What I am looking for is not out there; it is in me."* The second section introduces you to the mindset of money because where your attention goes your energy flows. We believe at least one of the reasons you are reading this book is to increase the abundance of the money you have. For this reason we have put some solid focus and powerful keys together to help you achieve your desired levels of income and assets. Lastly, we provide 26 additional action steps in the third section that help you uncover, unlock and unleash the success within you.

Read this book and reread it often. Zig Ziglar said *"People often say that motivation doesn't last. Well, neither does bathing – that's why we recommend it daily."* Implement the principles and start to live the life you want, the one you were divinely meant to have.

You may say that some of the secrets you will learn are just common sense but what I've found is that common sense isn't always common practice. Sometimes, it's just about awareness so keep an open mind, and know that successful people do what unsuccessful people won't or don't do!

My purpose is to empower and inspire others to live the life of their dreams in peace, joy, love and harmony. I encourage you to incorporate them as well and to achieve whatever it is you want in your life.

Enjoy the book, again come back to it as often as you can, share it with others and *Make it a Great Day*, every day!

Kevin Klimowski

MINDSET

**"You have within you right now,
everything you need to deal with whatever
the world can throw at you."**

Brian Tracy

- 1 -

TODAY IS THE FIRST DAY
OF THE REST OF YOUR LIFE

**"There are only 3 colors, 10 digits, and 7 notes;
It's what you do with them that's important."**

Jim Rohn

Success is like a combination lock, and once you know the numbers and the correct sequence they go in, the lock must open each and every time without fail. Your lock to your own success will be different than anyone else's, and even though the numbers may be the same, what makes your lock different is the sequence of the numbers. The *chapters or keys* in this book relate to the numbers of the combination to unlock the success in life that you have always dreamt of. It's now up to you to find your sequence.

Life is live, it's not a dress rehearsal, you can't take a Mulligan, and you can't TiVo or DVR it and replay it later, and you can't get it back to try again. It is happening right now, this very second. You can, however, choose to live it differently, perhaps even better from this second forward. The good news is that things are always changing and you, as the "Director of

You" can change your story anytime you want. Yes, you are both the Director and you play the leading role in your life which is appearing "live" right now, so take *ACTION*.

Today is literally the first day of the rest of your life. Now, choose how you're going to live it!

"If you don't design your own life plan, chances are you'll fall into someone else's plan. And guess what they have planned for you? Not much."

Jim Rohn

Think about it ... *your whole life changes the minute you change how you think and feel about your life!*

- 2 -

ATTITUDE IS EVERYTHING

**"There is little difference in people,
but that little difference makes a big difference.
The little difference is attitude.
The big difference is whether it is
positive or negative."**

W. Clement Stone

**"The minute you begin to change your attitude is
the minute you can begin to change your results."**

James Malinchak

Your attitude is the single most contributing factor to your success. Any obstacle, rejection, setback, challenging situation and adversity can be overcome with the right attitude. It will determine if you take action or make excuses, whether you keep going or quit, believe or doubt, agree or disagree and even win or lose.

Who you are today, what you have, what you do, where you've been and where you live are because of the actions you've taken and the excuses you've made. Your attitude about life, money, people, society, career, and everything is the bottom line cause of these effects.

> **"If you think you can do a thing or think you can't do a thing you're right."**
>
> *Henry Ford*

With a positive attitude, most people can cheerfully accomplish all the goals and tasks that are set out for them. They approach these goals like they approach all other aspects of their lives with confidence and conviction. These same people are passionate about what they do and see the good in all people.

With the right attitude you will have the ability to think clearly; be organized; motivate others to get involved; accomplish, meet and exceed goals; and strive to do better than you are at the present time.

> **"Nothing can stop the man with the right mental attitude from achieving his goal; nothing on earth can help the man with the wrong mental attitude."**
>
> *Thomas Jefferson*

People with positive attitudes are like "Thomas the Train" believing that they can do it; therefore they do. They walk through their daily lives believing "I think I can, I think I can, I think I can"; therefore "I do".

It's simple, negative attitude equals negative or limited results. Positive attitude equals positive and prosperous results. Success is an opinion and your attitude about your life determines your success.

"Work joyfully and peacefully, knowing that right thoughts and right efforts inevitably bring about right results."

James Allen

Think about it ... you can change your entire existence in a heartbeat just by changing your attitude!

- 3 -

TAKE 100% RESPONSIBILITY

"Responsibility is the price of greatness."

Winston Churchill

The event doesn't determine your outcome or response. The meaning you give the event is what determines your outcome or response.

It's time to stop the blaming, shaming, complaining, justifying, and wallowing in self pity and start taking 100% responsibility for your life. This is something I've learned from one of my mentors in life, Jack Canfield. In fact, it is one of the principles he covers in his book "The Success Principles".

"You are who you are today and will be who you will be tomorrow because of the actions you take and the excuses you make."

Kevin Klimowski

We've all been given pretty much the same opportunities in life. That's why some of the poorest of the poor have become the richest of the rich. These are the people who took advantage of the opportunities to become successful. Did they face adversity, roadblocks, failures and doubts? Sure. But instead of blaming others or life they took responsibility for themselves and achieved their level personal of success.

Life is full of examples of people who overcame disabilities, illness, challenges and setbacks. All too often in the world today there are people who never want to own up to their actions or even carry out their responsibilities. Once you reach a certain age in your life, you must carry on as an adult and dive head first into a world of important decisions. Especially when you think of life decisions that will mold your future, you must take complete responsibility for your actions and choices. You have to stop the justifying and blaming if you want to achieve any great level of success in your lifetime.

"We can let circumstances rule us, or we can take charge and rule our lives from within."

Earl Nightingale

Life is full of learning experiences. If you are not able to learn from mistakes you've made, then you are cheating yourself out of some of the most valuable of lessons. Character building comes from realizing you have made a mistake, owning up to any situation that you may have caused, and then finding the best possible way to make everything better again. People are quick to point the finger in order to get out of all kinds of sticky situations. However, it is the people who do not turn and run from their responsibilities that become great leaders, excellent parents and are successful in life.

Can society and the ever-intrusive media be the cause to the destruction of integrity and responsibility in the world, as we know it today? Of course! It is the knowing of just how you can do your part in order to make a change in the world that is most important.

Certainly we are all only human and it is within the nature of humanity to make mistakes. Looking back on your past, owning up to it and taking responsibility for yourself can help to eliminate repeat performances in the future. You are only one person, yet when you show others how to rise above, you are a force to be reckoned with.

"You must take personal responsibility.
You cannot change the circumstances,
the seasons, or the wind,
but you can change yourself.
That is something you have charge of."

Jim Rohn

Think about it ... only YOU can stop you or start you!

- 4 -

DEFINE YOUR LIFE PURPOSE

"Definiteness of purpose is the starting point of all achievement."

W. Clement Stone

Purpose is the motor that drives you to succeed; attitude is the fuel that keeps the motor running.

When you do what you love to do it may seem like you never work a day in your life. In order to find what you love to do you need to define your purpose. Many people find that looking for the purpose in their life is a struggle in itself. While you might think that this would be a simple question and answer process, there are a few things that you should consider when you are looking to define your life purpose. You can find your purpose and you may even find what some would consider being the secret to life. You just have to know where to look. The answer is simply inside your soul.

Your life purpose is about finding what you're passionate about and then a way to serve others with it. It really doesn't matter what you do as long as you enjoy doing it. Making yourself happy will have a trickledown effect to all of those people that are around you. Additionally, you will waste time looking for the meaning of life if you are completely unable to relax and enjoy yourself at least once in a while.

Success is an opinion and when you are "living on purpose", well, that could provide all the success you require in life.

"Singleness of purpose is one of the chief essentials for success in life, no matter what may be one's aim."

John D. Rockefeller

To define your purpose take some time alone in quiet meditation and ask yourself what it is you feel most passionate about. Stay there in that state until your subconscious mind gives you the answers you desire. Be patient with this process for the answers may or may not come quickly, but know eventually they will come.

If you're still finding it difficult to define your purpose ask others for help. Nobody has ever found true purpose in life by staying locked up at home and never taking the time to interact with others. People that are in your life are there to help you build a good level of communication and work you into a strong individual that can endure changes and growth in relationships. Ask them where they see your strengths and what contribution you provide to their lives.

"Life is a promise; fulfill it."

Mother Teresa

All in all, as you search for your life purpose it is extremely important that you never lose yourself along the way. Remaining true to who you are will help you see more clearly as you travel down your life's path. While you are exploring all of the things that are of interest to you, you may quickly gain a decent sense of where you need to be in the future. Remain organized, stay focused and never let yourself down and you should have no problem finding and defining the purpose in your life.

"There is one quality which one must possess to win, and that is definiteness of purpose, the knowledge of what one wants, and a burning desire to possess it."

Napoleon Hill

> ***Think about it ...*** *when you do what you love, you'll love what you do!*

For more information on discovering your life purpose and life purpose symbol, please contact the Success Coach Institute at 1-888-689-1130 or online at www.SuccessCoachInstitute.com.

- 5 -

FOCUS ON THE POSITIVE
IN EVERY SITUATION

**"A pessimist sees the difficulty in every opportunity;
an optimist sees the opportunity in every difficulty."**

Winston Churchill

Throughout history, there have been a number of great leaders. Many of these wonderful leaders had an incredibly positive outlook on life as well as the many life situations that can be thrown your way. However, it can be difficult at times to wade through all of the stress and pessimistic thoughts that are all too prevalent with everyday life. In order to cut through all of this negative energy, you should learn how to focus on some of the more positive things in life. Taking each situation as it comes your way and spinning it in a positive light will help you to grow and prosper as a well-rounded individual.

Have you ever heard someone talk about the laws of attraction? This theory focuses on the idea that if you dream about something or focus your attention on it long enough, then you will receive or attain it. Now, if you are constantly looking at the negative side of the spectrum as you go through life, the chances are very good that you will end up having a string of less than desirable events come your way. Instead of letting stress and worry run your life, see the light at the end of the tunnel and the beauty in the little things. You may just be amazed at the outcome!

Besides, the only benefit about the negative in a situation is to learn what not to do or how you can do it differently in the future, that's it. You can't change the event once it happened, you can only learn from it and move on. Plus, focusing on the negative usually makes you feel bad about yourself, how empowered will you be to achieve your goals in that state?

Remember the saying, "every cloud has a silver lining"? If you go about every day making it your goal to point out some of the good things in life, then you will end up rewarding yourself with lots of positive energy. Whether you choose to believe it all the time or not, there is something good that comes from every situation. Change happens for a reason. Even if there is something sudden that comes about in your life such as a loss of a job, a bankruptcy, the death of a loved one or even a grave illness, it will benefit you to realize that everything happens for a reason.

On the other side of the spectrum, there are always people who make their way through life with a smile on their face. Now, it goes without saying that not every single day can be joyful and fun-filled. Yet, those people who smile each and every day tend to have a happier and much more positive outlook on life. Good things truly do come to good people; sometimes you simply have to wait for it to be your turn!

Remain positive and never forget to be happy for the good things in life that you do have. When you have a good career or business, make sure that you put forth 100% effort each day. As you love, be certain to love those people in your life like it is your last day on earth. After all, when your last day does come, you want people to look back positively on everything that you were and all that you achieved in life.

> **"All that you accomplish or fail to accomplish with your life is the direct result of your thoughts."**
>
> *James Allen*

Think about it ... the choice is always yours as to what you focus on; the positive or the negative, and just remember which one will move you forward and which one will hold you back!

- 6 -

PRACTICE POSITIVE SELF-TALK

**"You are today where your
thoughts have brought you;
you will be tomorrow where your
thoughts take you."**

James Allen

If you take the "t" out of can't and won't, you'll be amazed at what you can and will do.

How you think is how you act. What you think is what you do. What you have achieved is a direct result of how you have thought, how you think, and/or what you say to yourself. We are what we think about or say to ourselves most of the time. Our self-talk is the major deciding factor to what we have, what we do and what we lack or don't have in life. Negative disempowering thoughts produce negative results, lack, unhappiness, and things in life we don't like, want or have.

You see you can have, achieve and accomplish anything you truly desire and want in your life, just by controlling what you say and think to yourself. Positive empowering thoughts and words will bring about more of what you want, feel or desire in your life.

Have you ever found that you were in a situation where you were talking to yourself and found it to be negative or you were putting yourself down? If so, then you should know that you are not alone when it comes to negative self-talk. Everybody talks to them selves each and every day. Is yours positive or negative self-talk? You have a choice to make and the great thing is you are able to give yourself a huge pep talk whenever you find it necessary, so why not make it a positive one!

"The mind is everything. What you think you become."

Buddha

If you stop to think about it, you can and should be your very own cheerleader. You know who you are, and talking positively to yourself throughout your day can help you in many, many ways. Additionally, positive self-talk can be an incredible way to work through any number of issues that are coming your way. As a matter of fact, you may just find that positive self-talk will be the best way that you can take control over your life and make it work so that you can remain on a path for success and happiness.

As a human being, there is just no way to avoid many of the challenges that you will need to face. In a nutshell, difficulties and problems that arise for you to overcome are simply a part of life. Finding great ways such as a pep talk in the shower or telling yourself out loud that you can get through the financial or business challenges you may be having can have incredible power over your outcome. The next time that you find something in your life is simply spiraling out of control; take a moment to talk yourself into a positive, optimistic way of thinking.

If you have ever worked with meditation or affirmations, you may already know a couple of motivational statements that you can use when you wake up first thing in the morning. Starting off the day by telling yourself that you are a great person and that you will achieve great things can help you to project the kind of results that you desire in life. Before you know it, your entire outlook through positive self-talk will help to bring you a wealth of happiness. Any wise man can tell you that there is no problem that is too large to overcome, however the truly successful person will be sure to tell you that with positive self-talk you can literally handle any challenge.

"To do things in a way you want to do them, you will have to acquire the ability to think the way you want to think; this is the first step toward getting rich."

Wallace D. Wattles

Think about it ... stop using your stinking thinking and negative words against you, and start using your positive thoughts and encouraging words to create what you want in your life!

- 7 -

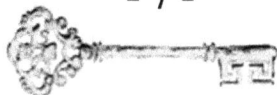

BELIEVE TO ACHIEVE

**"Man is made by his belief.
As he believes, so he is."**

Johann Wolfgang von Goethe

It happens all too often that people seem to lose focus on the dreams and goals that they have simply because there are too many stresses or difficulties going on within their personal lives. However, if you are able to keep a positive spin on everything that comes your way you are going to have a much easier time keeping your eye on the prize and achieving everything that is important to you in your lifetime. Start with your mind and focus on what you really want to attain in your life. Once your mind is clear, then your successes in life are sure to follow.

Sometimes we as humans are our own worst enemy. We limit ourselves because of all the doubt and skepticism we feed ourselves about what we can and can't accomplish. But, once you give yourself over to the fact that you can achieve anything in life and install that belief as a habit, you will see the pot of gold at the end of your rainbow.

Napoleon Hill stated it best, *"Whatever the mind of man can conceive and believe it can achieve"*. And with that belief in themselves millions of people have accomplished great things in their lives. You can literally do just about anything you set out to do, but until you start to believe in yourself and your abilities life will continually be a struggle. However, once you truly give every fiber of your being to this concept, a whole new world of possibilities will unfold.

Are you even aware of your true potential? Unfortunately, there are too many people who simply do not believe in themselves enough to achieve everything that they want in life. Once you are able to realize that you have everything it takes to be successful, you can become your own biggest fan. Certainly, success is sure to follow once you are able to realize your potential and path for success.

Do you remember we talked about the 'Little Engine That Could' in chapter two? The phrase "I think I can, I think I can". The wonderful thing is that even if you have always been a pessimist, there is never anything holding you back from changing your outlook on life. No matter where you are in your life's path, you can work to better yourself and believe in order to achieve everything that you want.

Believing in yourself and the ideas and goals that you have set forth can help you to bring amazing things your way. All that you have to do is set the proper goals in front of you, think positively and you can be well on your way to complete and total success and happiness for yourself and all of your friends and loved ones.

"The thing always happens
that you really believe in;
and the belief in a thing
makes it happen."

Frank Lloyd Wright

Think about it ... the only person stopping you from achieving all you want is you, and whether you believe you can or can't. So, believe and you will achieve!

Our Gift To You!

Receive a free copy of Napolean Hill's book, "Think and Grow Rich" with our compliments by sending an email to library@afabulousgroup.com - Just type FREE HILL BOOK in the subject line and we'll send it to you!

- 8 -

DREAM BIG DREAMS

**"Dream no small dreams for they
have no power to move the hearts of men."**

Johann Wolfgang von Goethe

There are many things in life that you may have dreams about. You may want to find and follow a new career path or maybe it has even been your lifelong dream to start a business, write a book or achieve financial freedom.

Unfortunately, all too many people end up giving up on their dreams when life starts to deal them a difficult hand. Some people will remain financially unstable or live from paycheck to paycheck without even a glimmer of hope that their financial outlook will soon change. It is these people who are sadly living without their dream. You see, once you lose your dream then you have no big life goals to reach for. Since life can pass you by in the blink of an eye, it is imperative that you start to reopen those dreams that you had in days gone by. Once you open up yourself to your dreams about life, love, health, finances and the future, then you're going to see a whole new world of possibilities opening up for you.

**"Winners, I am convinced,
imagine their dreams first.
They want it with all their heart and
expect it to come true.
There is, I believe, no other way to live."**

Joe Montana

Let's say your dream is to be financially stable. Well, why not start to dream even bigger by setting a goal of financial independence. Any successful person will be able to tell you that if you can dream it, then you can be it. Realizing your dreams may be as simple as believing in yourself and your goals. Once you have a true dream and the belief that you can follow those goals through, you will be able to reap the rewards that are laid out for you at the end of your journey.

You may run across people all the time in your life that you simply cannot believe the obstacles that they overcome on a regular basis. Perhaps it is somebody with a disability or a person that grew up poor and is now rich. Maybe someone you knew who was bankrupt and now is financially secure. The people who will move forward in life and persevere through obstacles such as these are the ones who have really big dreams and most likely a positive approach to realizing them. After all, if you are not holding onto your dreams and dreaming big, then all you have are hopeless days and nights.

Your dreams are like the fuel that gives you the energy to achieve your desired level of success. No dreams, no fuel. Small dreams, little fuel to get you where you want, but big dreams give you all the fuel you need to keep going no matter how far the destination.

"I like thinking big.
If you're going to be thinking anything,
you might as well think big."

Donald Trump

Throughout life, you can take the easy way out. However, in order to realize your goals, you truly have to dream big in order to dance through all of the highs and lows that are thrown your way.

"High achievers spot rich opportunities swiftly, make big decisions quickly and move into action immediately. Follow these principles and you can make your dreams come true."

Robert H. Schuller

> ***Think about it*** ... *if you're going to dream then you might as well dream BIG because it doesn't take any more time or effort, does it?*

- 9 -

HAVE FAITH AND TRUST

"Faith is taking the first step,
even when you can't see the whole staircase."

Martin Luther King Jr.

When you have faith and trust in yourself you believe you are going to have an incredible level of success. That belief now gives you confidence. Confidence is a truly amazing thing and you are able to conquer just about anything. There are plenty of people out there who have a good amount of confidence in others; they just simply need to work on themselves in order to be able to enjoy true success in both their personal and professional lives.

Having faith and trust is knowing that you have all you need to be who you want to be, and to be who you already are. It's accepting that when things don't necessarily go your way, that you have the confidence to push on and find a different course of action. With faith and trust you know in your heart of hearts that God, the Universe or a higher power wants the absolute best for you and that things always happen for a reason. It knows that your creator would never put you in a situation that you couldn't eventually overcome. It's believing in yourself that you can do anything you put your mind to.

So are we born with 'faith and trust' traits? Not exactly. While you have a certain amount of trust in your parents as a baby and young child that they will take care of you, there are certain events that can take place in your life that will hinder this feeling of trust or confidence. You then find yourself working to build up that faith and trust all over again. Unfortunately, faith and trust may get broken so many times in your life that you may end up building up a wall or becoming toughened to the idea that you can have complete confidence in yourself as well as others.

The ability to believe in your self is amazing. When you think that you can do anything that you put your mind to then you are going to be able to achieve great things. You are going to make a number of mistakes along the way, of course. It is the ability to pick yourself up and dust off that will help you to build up your confidence as well as your character. Doing what is right for you and right for your chosen path will be the best way to achieve all of your goals.

> **"To believe in the things you can see and touch is no belief at all.**
> **But to believe in the unseen is both a triumph and a blessing."**
>
> *Bob Proctor*

Some of our best leaders have had the faith and trust in them selves as well as with our world that helped them become who they are. A good leader is a person who has the confidence to make decisions for the good of the people they are in charge of.

Additionally, they will be able to change and adjust in a way that will benefit everyone that is involved.

In your business life, you need to have faith and trust that you are doing the best that you possibly can. You are never going to achieve a high level of success if you do not have the faith and trust in yourself that you are worthy of such success. The same idea goes for your path in your personal life as well.

Think of all of the situations in your professional life where you have to make decisions or exude a certain level of confidence in order to excel. You need to have the faith, trust and self-confidence that will set you above all of the competition that is standing in your way. Once you fully believe in yourself, then you will succeed. It is that simple.

"Believe in yourself!
Have faith in your abilities!
Without a humble but reasonable confidence in
your own powers you cannot be
successful or happy."

Norman Vincent Peale

Think about it *... if you have faith you can't have fear; the two can't exist together at the same time!*

- 10 -

DON'T SET LIMITS ON YOURSELF

"The only limits in our life are those we impose on ourselves."

Bob Proctor

Have you ever been told that you simply cannot do something, but yet you try over and over again until you can finally achieve it? If so, then you are more than likely a strong person that does not like to settle for "no" as an answer. Good for you! However, there are a large number of people who only work to their ability based on what they are told they can accomplish.

Knowing that you are limited in some way, shape or form is one thing. Accepting that you are limited in any way is a whole other ball game altogether. You can be told that you have limits or that your abilities will only take you so far, but if you work hard enough you will surprise yourself fully.

Sadly, there are a large number of people who lock themselves away under the thought process that they will never be more than they are today. You may know somebody that you work with who never goes for that promotion or will not strive to work on a project that seems hopeless to many. It is unfortunate that these people do not have the drive or self-belief that they can be more than they are in any given situation. For yourself, you need to always set the bar higher and higher. It will only be then that you realize your true potential in life as well as the ability to succeed at no matter what you put your mind to.

> ## "There are no limits to the mind except those we acknowledge."
>
> *Napoleon Hill*

You may however; set goals only as big as you believe you have the capability to achieve. Many people limit themselves because they don't currently know how to do anymore, so they never achieve the things they truly desire. Keep in mind that you know more today than you knew 5, 10, or even 20 years ago. You have accomplished things today you never knew you could 20 years ago because you have never stopped learning. Remember that as you plan for your future. You are going to know a lot more in 20 years from now so just because you don't know everything you need to do or every action you need to take to reach a goal today, please don't let that limit you from setting big goals. Believe you can reach it and beyond, and trust the knowledge; the 'how to' will come.

> ## "There is no limit to the ingenuity of man if it is properly and vigorously applied under conditions of peace and justice."
>
> *Winston Churchill*

Self-esteem also seems to play a very important role in the types of limits that you set for yourself. If you are a person with low self-esteem then you may wind up thinking that you are right in the place that you deserve to be in. To help build better self-esteem, you should start off by working on smaller self-goals and using small success you have had to build confidence. Before you know it, you will start accomplishing things that you never dreamed to be possible before. The sky is truly the limit as long as you believe that it is.

"Aim for the moon. If you miss, you may hit a star."

W. Clement Stone

Do you have a dream? If so, then it is crucial that you work for it. Some of our greatest leaders and inventors looked at what they were told their limits were and simply would not accept them. Pushing themselves further and working toward a bigger dream is what made them into great leaders and inventors. In order to get the best from yourself you have to strive to be the best.

"Never tell me the sky's the limit when there are footprints on the moon."

Unknown

> ***Think about it ...*** *your inner life is what determines your outer life. If you are limiting your thoughts and goals to what you know, how can you grow?*

- 11 -

ELIMINATE LIMITING BELIEFS

**"What we can or cannot do,
what we consider possible or impossible,
is rarely a function of our true capability.
It is more likely a function of
our beliefs about who we are."**

Anthony Robbins

Do you realize that you could end up being one of your biggest adversaries without even realizing it? There are a whole lot of people in this world who are their own worst critics. These are the people who will end up stopping themselves from following their dreams simply because they are afraid to go forward. You need to take some notes about the laws of attraction and realize that if you start to think more positively and start to envision your life with the goals that you want then you are much more likely to attract those things.

Basically speaking, the only limits that you are going to face in your life are the ones that you set on yourself. You are the one that is holding yourself back from greatness. Once you realize this, then you can persevere and become the person that you have always dreamt about.

Beliefs are the foundation that supports you just like the foundation of a house or building. For that structure to remain standing and stable it needs a solid foundation under it. You're beliefs work pretty much the same way. If you have limiting beliefs they're like a weak foundation and will never be able to support the life you dream of. Your limiting beliefs will stop you cold in your tracks when trying to accomplish a goal.

But, how do you eliminate limiting beliefs? The first step is awareness. Simply become aware that you have beliefs that are limiting you from achieving things you desire. Second is finding out why you have that particular belief, what was it in your past that started that belief. Was it something somebody said or did to you? Third, just accept it and acknowledge it for what it is. Fourth, realize that your past does not equal your future. Of course you can't change the past and what occurred or happened, but understand that that was then, and this is now. Fifth, create affirmations to recondition your subconscious mind and repeat them over and over until the new empowering belief is established. More on affirmations is covered in chapter 31.

Now, sit back and think about the thoughts that may have crossed your mind over the past few days or even weeks. Have you ever told yourself "Well, I don't know why I bother because I can't do that anyway." People are always stuck in the mode of thinking that they are too fat or not smart enough or even good enough to get the things that they want. Why is this? Why are people stuck into limiting themselves and following the belief that they cannot be anything better than the limits that they set on their own life?

One could look at their parents or teachers from their childhood, their peers or society today and even the media and say that this is a good reason why people fall victim to limiting beliefs. Because if people tell you that you are too fat or that you are too slow or not good enough, eventually you will start to focus on the negative instead of the positive things in your life. Unfortunately, when this happens then you run the risk of never making it anywhere.

On the other hand, you can be mostly to blame for limiting beliefs taking over your mind. You need to give yourself a slap to wake up and tell yourself that you are good enough or that you are smart enough to move toward your life's goals. True happiness will come when you no longer let limiting beliefs run your life.

> **"Strong beliefs win strong men,**
> **and then make them stronger."**
>
> *Richard Bach*

Think about it ... decisions move you forward, excuses only hold you back. And excuses are caused by one thing, your limiting beliefs. Change your beliefs, stop the excuses, never quit and achieve you goals!

- 12 -

FACE YOUR FEARS

"Too many of us are not living our dreams because we are living our fears."

Les Brown

There could be any number of things in your life that you are afraid of. You may have a phobia, a fear of public speaking, a fear of failure or you could simply have a fear of commitment when it comes to relationships. In general, each and every one of us has something that we are afraid of. However, there are only a few of us that have the strength and courage to face our fears head on.

The thing is, when you have a fear you really need to be able to recognize it. If you go throughout life refusing to admit that you are afraid of something, then all you are doing is pretty much sweeping this issue under the rug. No matter what the fear may be, finding the source and subsequently the ways that you can work on eliminating it will be your best bet towards freedom. After all, when you are stuck in fear, then you are slowly becoming a prisoner of this thought or feeling. The only way that you will be able to move past the fear is to embrace it, suck it up, face it and then do it anyway.

"Fears are nothing more than a state of mind."

Napoleon Hill

Fear to speak in public and the failure to take risks happen to be two of the most common fears that people have alongside a fear of creepy crawlies such as snakes and spiders. However, the failure to take risks in life can be one of the most powerful fears when you are talking about things that can hold you back. Not that you have to take a major gamble on huge decisions in life in order to face this fear, this is still a debilitating fear none the less and it should be addressed accordingly.

Another strong fear people have is the fear of rejection. Fear of rejection is negative internal self-talk. It is not what anyone says or does to you. It is what you say or do when they stop. Eleanor Roosevelt said, *"No one can make me feel inferior without my permission."*

One of the easiest ways to deal with the fear of rejection is to realize that you didn't have what you wanted before you asked. So, if someone says 'no' to your request, you're still no worse off, because you didn't have it before you asked and you still don't have it after you asked, nothing changed. Remember, people are not rejecting you; they're rejecting the offer or opportunity.

The first step in facing your fears would have to be recognition. After you know what your fears are you can then investigate what the reasons may be as to why these fears are even infesting your head. Once you think you have determined the cause, there are a number of different ways that you can attack your fears and face them head on.

Nobody ever got over a fear by simply snapping his or her fingers. Set some goals that are sure to help you deal with your fear step by step. Also, it's best not to go at it alone. Address your fears with a therapist, your success coach, mentor, accountability partner and/or mastermind group (more on this chapters 45 and 46) and ask for their support in helping you identify the obstacle and overcome the fear. Additionally, there are always your family members, colleagues and friends that you have by your side to help you along. Having a great support system in place will help you down the path of controlling and then eliminating any fears that you may have whether they are personal or business in nature.

> **"Inaction breeds doubt and fear.**
> **Action breeds confidence and courage.**
> **If you want to conquer fear,**
> **do not sit home and think about it.**
> **Go out and get busy."**
>
> *Dale Carnegie*

Think about it ... when you face your fears, take action against them, the fears just go away!

- 13 -

EMBRACE THE 'NO'

"Get used to the idea that there is going to be a lot of rejection along the way to the gold ring. The secret to success is to not give up. When someone says no, you say, 'Next!'

Jack Canfield

When faced with rejection remember 'SWSWSWSW', some will, some won't, so what, someone's waiting. Rejection or 'no' is not 'no,' it is just not now!

Throughout your life, there are going to be plenty of times where you will suffer from dealing with some sort of rejection. Unfortunately, if you are not taught the proper set of skills in order to deal with rejection then you may find a difficulty getting over the feelings that will come over you. From a very young age, you may find yourself being rejected by other children whether it is on the playground or in a classroom setting. Social skills will be one way that you can deal with rejection; however inner strength will be the ultimate aid as you learn to embrace rejection throughout life.

If you have ever felt rejection, then on some level you may have endured a great level of pain as well. Rejection that comes in the form of a romantic relationship can be quite devastating no matter what age you are. It is crucial that you are able to feel the pain and subsequently learn to work through it. Feeling the pain will bring you another step closer to realizing that you are able to overcome it instead of letting the emotional pain take over your heart and soul.

> **"I take rejection as someone blowing a bugle in my ear to wake me up and get going, rather than retreat."**
>
> *Sylvester Stallone*

When it comes to rejection in the business world, all too many people never learn how to properly deal with the loss of an important job or failure to even obtain a dream job, being turned down for a business loan, rejection from a publisher, having a business close or a prospect say 'no' to a sale. Simply understand that rejection is a part of the life process. Not everybody will want what you offer or think your idea is as great as you do, so what.

Have you ever had the chance to listen in on some form of motivational speaking session or seminar? If you have, then you have probably heard all about realizing your dreams, learning to cope with rejection and how to pick yourself up, dust off and go on with your goals. These are all incredibly valuable things to learn about and in turn are wonderful keys to take with you not only in your business life but your personal life as well.

Many people are truly amazed at the power of knowing that they have the ability to talk themselves through just about anything. Life is too short to dwell on things that you cannot change. Your success is something that you can have complete control over, especially when you learn how to embrace rejection and bring all of your dreams to reality with a good amount of determination on your part.

"The ultimate measure of a man is not where he stands in moments of comfort and convenience, but where he stands at times of challenge and controversy."

Martin Luther King Jr.

Think about it ... people are not rejecting you personally. They're rejecting the idea, offer or opportunity. Not everyone will want what you offer, remember there are 6 billion people in this world, however a lot of them will. Embrace rejection and go find them!

- 14 -

USE SMALL SUCCESSES
TO CREATE MOMENTUM
AND CONFIDENCE

**"To establish true self-esteem
we must concentrate on our successes
and forget about the failures and
the negatives in our lives."**

Denis Waitley

You know that you have a dream of being successful, and you may even have a great plan in place that is meant to help you realize your dreams of success. However, there are a certain amount of steps that you need to take along the way. Nobody ever wakes up in the morning and says "I'm going to become rich and famous today" and to actually have it come true by dinner time. It is imperative that you take things in stride and learn how you can use the small successes to your advantage by letting them help you create momentum and confidence.

Whether you realize it or not no matter your age you have had so many successes in your life that you should appreciate, be proud of and use as momentum to achieve greater things. In fact writing down your successes can be an empowering way to build confidence when faced with a difficult task, challenge or roadblock you face toward a goal. When you think and start to believe that you can't do something use your past successes to propel you forward. After all, there are a number of smaller successes that you will reach on your way to your goal of greatness that are worth celebrating. The sooner you recognize them, the better your path for the future will be. Guaranteed!

Have you ever stepped back and thought to yourself that it is just impossible for you to achieve everything that you would like to do? If so, then this is extremely unfortunate. All too often, people will look past the wonderful small successes in life instead of using them as a great way to build confidence and help to drive you to keep on pushing harder and harder. If you really stop to think about it, these tiny successes have a huge impact on your life. You just have to be able to see them, appreciate them and celebrate them accordingly.

Did you know that once you have a clear picture of your future and what is to come, you are going to be able to knock down all of the obstacles in your way with ease? Clarity is a wonderful thing to have when you have a huge goal that you are striving for. The little successes that you will meet along this path to greatness will help you to see even clearer as you go along. If you believe that you can be successful and you have a clear vision of what you want and how you are going to get there, then there is nothing that can get in your way and stop you from success.

Instead of pushing aside all of your accomplishments in life because you cannot seem to stop and smell the roses, you need to learn how to have the proper amount of focus. If you are able to focus on positive things in your life, then good things will come your way. If you only focus on the negative, then the good things that happen to you in your life will not matter as much as they should. Remain focused and celebrate the small successes in life.

"The ladder of success is best climbed by stepping on the rungs of opportunity."

Ayn Rand

We challenge you to take action on this concept immediately. Take out a sheet of paper and list a minimum of 30 successes you have had in your life. Some examples could be as simple as you have woken up every day of your life, a book you read, and you got your driver's license. Just list as many successes, big or small that come to your mind. Heck, you can even list you passed 1st, 2nd, or 3rd grade. Those are all successes. When you do this exercise I know you will start to be energized by all that you have accomplished. Next, appreciate your successes, because so often we take them for granted. You'll even begin to notice how things at one time seemed so difficult or overwhelming today you do with ease. What once was hard is now easy!

**"The first and most important step
toward success is the feeling that we can succeed."**

Nelson Boswell

***Think about it* ...** *there is no
such thing as a small success!*

- 15 -

PATIENCE IS A VIRTUE

"Money grows on the tree of patience."

Japanese Proverb

In your life it may seem that all you seem to do is hurry up and then wait. There are many milestones that you look forward to achieving, however it seems like it can take forever for you to get to them. Why is it that people say that 'patience is a virtue?' and often times it's the last thing that you want to hear when you are longing for something to happen. So, how can you go through life with a good understanding of patience as well as how you can practice it?

Many people get tired of waiting. Whether you are waiting on a decision for a big sale, in line at the grocery store or you have been waiting for a long time to start a new career or business, waiting can be frustrating. Sometimes, you may even find yourself getting bored or angry while you wait, depending on the given situation. What you may not be realizing is that you can end up adding a great deal of unwanted stress to your life. Worrying and frustration are two feelings that can have a profound effect on your body, emotional state as well as your level of success.

When you are impatient, then you are actually missing out on a number of wonderful things that are going on around you in life. Whether you realize it or not, you can end up going through life stressed out and not dealing with the here and now simply because you cannot wait a second longer. In addition to the stresses and pieces of life that you are missing out on, you are also walking a fine line that could result in harm to yourself or others around you because you are rushing and not taking care of each situation in the here and now. Rushing projects to completion can lead to many errors and mistakes both in judgment and correctness.

In order for you to avoid errors, you must adopt an outlook on life that includes patience and the ability to take life as it comes. Living in the moment can have amazing benefits; you simply have to want it. When you are able to live in the present, you will find that you have a much stronger appreciation for the little things in life. Because you are not rushing ahead, you are going to see that the people, places and things that surround you are a huge part of the person that you are today, not who you think is coming in the future.

As you look at patience and the level that you have or do not have, you are going to find that you can live a life that is free of anxiety if you simply put your mind to it. When you feel better and you are less stressed, you will be able to think clearly and more creatively on the goals you want to accomplish. Less cares and worries can make for a calm, happy, successful individual. Patience truly is a virtue; you simply have to use patience to your advantage.

"Patience is something you admire in the driver behind you, but not in the one ahead."

Bill McGlashen

Think about it ... *good things come to those who wait. Be patient, be dedicated and be persistent on your path to excellence!*

- 16 -

SUCCESS LEAVES CLUES:
LEARN FROM OTHERS BEFORE YOU

**"No one lives long enough to learn everything
they need to learn starting from scratch.
To be successful, we absolutely, positively have to
find people who have already paid the price
to learn the things that we need to learn
to achieve our goals."**

Brian Tracy

In 1954 Roger Bannister was the first person to break the four-minute mile. The next year over a dozen other people also did it. Something that hadn't been done before in history is now common practice. Why? Because success leaves many clues and just because you haven't done something yet, doesn't mean it can't be done. All you need to do is find someone who has done what you want and do exactly what they did to achieve it. Follow their blueprint; mirror their pattern. Certainly, you know plenty of people who you can look to and you will see their level of success. These people have worked hard to get where they are and you can look at them as shining examples of what you could be if you tried.

Do you think that some of the successful people that have come before you have suffered from mixed thoughts of themselves or doubts in their abilities? Of course! However, they were able to look past these negative thoughts and feelings in order to focus on persevering and reaching all of their goals. Personal success and success in the business world will only come to you if you can take notes from the people who have succeeded before you in cutting all of the negative thoughts out of their path.

"If you want to be successful, find someone who has achieved the results you want and copy what they did and you'll achieve the same results."

Anthony Robbins

Libraries and bookstores are filled with books of people who have achieved great things and overcame what at the time seemed to be insurmountable obstacles. Their whole history of achievement is laid out there for you to learn from. If you put your hand in a pot of honey some of it will stick. Reading is no different, read a motivational or self help book and some of it will stick.

Life is truly a journey and you may find a good number of people that you can look up to along the way. You can find people in your life or through books and seminars that you can look up to that will become a great source of strength and inspiration that will be a wonderful asset to have. Along the way, never beat yourself up for any of the mistakes that you make and do not be afraid to talk out your thoughts and feelings with those people in your life that you look up to.

"That some achieve great success, is proof to all that others can achieve it as well."

Abraham Lincoln

Take your life one step at a time. You cannot achieve great success unless you take each goal as it comes and then work on toward the next one. There may be any number of obstacles that you will need to overcome, so take some cues from the successful people who you can think of and look at some of the clues that they left behind. You can use these clues to set a solid structure in place for the foundation of your own success. Throughout your journey in life and the successes that you are longing for, you can learn a great deal from just about everyone that you meet. Life is a learning process and you have to be aware of everything surrounding you in order to make it.

Think about it ... you can achieve whatever you want in life. Just find someone who has done exactly what you want, do exactly what they did to achieve it and you could end up with the exact same results or something better for you!

- 17 -

NEVER QUIT BECAUSE QUITTERS NEVER WIN AND WINNERS NEVER QUIT

"I hated every minute of training, but I said, don't quit. Suffer now and live the rest of your life as a champion."

Muhammad Ali

You'll never fail if you never quit because only two things can happen; one you'll succeed or two you'll die trying.

If you have ever felt like you just cannot go on any longer, probably the last thing that you want to hear someone telling you is that winners never quit. After all, you are already down on your luck and giving up may be the best sounding option in your mind. However, shouldn't you be taking the words about never quitting and using them to help motivate you through your issues? If you think about it, unless you try and never give up, you will never know exactly what is waiting for you at the end.

**"Some people fold after making
one timid request. They quit too soon.
Keep asking until you find the answers.
In sales there are usually four or five "no's"
before you get a "yes."**

Jack Canfield

When you feel that you need some motivation to help keep you moving forward, you may want to look at some of the success stories that surround you. Not one person on this planet ever reached a level of great success because they quit. Everyone has challenges along the way to achieving their goals, but the ones who achieve their goals find the inner strength, motivation and determination to keep pushing though.

**"Success seems to be connected with action.
Successful people keep moving.
They make mistakes, but they don't quit."**

Conrad Hilton

Do you remember that old saying that goes … *"If at first you don't succeed, try, try again?"* If so, then you may want to fold it up, place it in your pocket and hold onto it for a challenging or rainy day. You are never alone when it comes to wanting to give up on occasion. Absolutely everyone on this planet has wanted to give up on something and quit at least once in their lifetime. Many of the greatest inventors of the world have given us some seriously amazing gifts, simply because they would never give up on their notion or dream. You too can live by the idea that you should never quit and you might just be amazed at how your life will turn out.

63

"Once you learn to quit, it becomes a habit."

Vince Lombardi

Disappointment is obviously a huge part in growing up. However, when you take the steps to make sure that you are not contributing to your own disappointment, then better things are going to come your way. By keeping strong and persevering through whatever comes your way, you are also going to be able to remain a strong positive influence on the other people surrounding you in your life.

There is never any end to the challenges that may cross your path. The difference is … a quitter will stay behind, whereas a person who never gives up will simply find a way to get on with life, leaving each and every quitter in the dust.

**"Pain is temporary.
It may last a minute, or an hour, or a day,
or a year, but eventually it will subside and
something else will take its place.
If I quit, however, it lasts forever."**

Lance Armstrong

Think about it … if you hadn't quit in the past on something that was important for you to accomplish where would you be right now? Never quit!

- 18 -

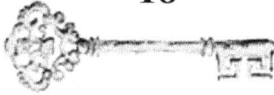

COMMIT TO EXCELLENCE

"Excellence is an art won by training and habituation. We do not act rightly because we have virtue or excellence, but we rather have those because we have acted rightly. We are what we repeatedly do. Excellence, then, is not an act but a habit."

Aristotle

Success starts with attitude and is achieved with commitment and perseverance.

Do you know that you were put on this planet to do great things? While it may not always seem like you are able to excel in the manner that you would like to, we all have a purpose in life. Some folks were put here in order to bring communities together while others were born into this life in order to create medicines that will heal the sick. We all have a purpose. In order for you to find your purpose in this great thing that we call life, you must first become dedicated. Find your path as you commit to excellence.

You should know that you are never going to be successful at anything unless you put your mind to it. There could be a number of amazing things out there that you can accomplish, however if you do not try then you will never succeed. A commitment to excellence simply means giving it your all, being all you can be, never settling for second best and always striving to be a better person.

When it comes to your personal life, you can commit to excellence by always staying true to yourself and showing others exactly who you are on the inside. Work hard to build strong relationships and never settle for anything less than truth, honesty and integrity. People who have a good level of commitment to excellence are usually quite popular with the general public and are able to easily forge partnerships and relationships with a great number of people.

As you think of commitment to excellence in a professional setting, this is a goal that you can set in order to really put yourself above all of the competition that may stand in your way. Focusing on your goal and sticking with it should be your main priority. Nobody is saying that you have to be perfect. Everyone can tell you that there really is no such thing as perfection. However, you can truly strive to put your best effort forward going into each and every project or task that you take on.

There are a number of businesses and corporations out there who like to use the phrase commitment to excellence as their motto, even professional sports team use it. While these words sound great on paper, if they are not meeting the needs and expectations of their customer base or being all they can be, then the words really mean nothing. When you strive for the best, you have to work at it. It is really that simple.

Sure, there are people out there who do not have to do much work to become successful because they were either born into money or they got lucky. However, you cannot measure success or excellence by the number of zeros that there are in your bank account. True success can be measured by the good things that you do in life for yourself as well as others around you.

"Desire is the key to motivation, but its determination and commitment to an unrelenting pursuit of your goal - a commitment to excellence - that will enable you to attain the success you seek."

Mario Andretti

Commit to yourself. Commit to others. Commit to excellence. Everything else will just simply fall in line.

"If you don't have the time to do it right, then how will you have the time to do it over?"

Jodi Nicholson

Think about it ... without a total commitment to excellence you are robbing yourself and the world of what you are truly capable of!

- II -

MONEY

**"Money saved is
as good as money earned."**

Danish Proverb

19

TO EARN MORE, YOU HAVE TO LEARN MORE

"In today's knowledge-based economy, what you earn depends on what you learn."

William J. Clinton

Do you remember being younger, when you were in grade school? The chances are very good that both your elders and your teachers all told you that you can never learn too much. This is a great thought to live by, especially when you think of the simple fact that you learn something new each and every day. Whether you are a person who likes to read books and magazines or you are going back to school to study for a new career, the possibilities of knowledge are virtually endless.

In today's day and age, we are surrounded by all sorts of different and incredibly, easy-to-use, ways that we can gather information to learn more. The internet alone has given us a whole new wealth of knowledge right at our fingertips. No matter where you turn today, you can quench your thirst for knowledge.

Now more than ever people are looking for new and interesting ways that they can make money, either with a new career or work on the side that they can use to supplement their current income. Knowledge is certainly power and when you learn more you are certainly going to be able to earn more. As a matter of fact, many employers today will offer pay increases for their employees who complete various classes in their relative field. The more classes you take the higher potential you have for the money that you can generate. Even if you find yourself stuck in a dead end job, there is no limit to the career possibilities that can open up once you take the necessary steps to learn.

"Formal education will make you a living; self-education will make you a fortune."

Jim Rohn

When you are speaking of the various ways that you can earn money, what you will learn rather quickly is that there is simply no way for you to get rich quick unless you win the lottery. Everything else will take a little bit of finesse on your part. Can you make money quickly with a smart internet plan? Of course you can, however in order to do so you will need to learn a little bit more about your potential in terms of financial earnings as well as all of the ins and outs of the internet plan you are thinking of venturing into.

The internet has opened up a whole new world for people who are business minded and looking to become an entrepreneur. If you have the drive and the means, then you too can be well on your way to a lifelong dream of financial freedom and knowledge that will take your career to a whole new level. Furthermore, once you have learned how to make money with

71

your new knowledge, you can then look into learning even further with the different ways that you can invest your money and make it work even harder for you.

Go to seminars, attended workshops, read books, listen to CD's everything you want to know is out there for you to learn.

**"Live as if you were to die tomorrow.
Learn as if you were to live forever."**

Mohandas Gandhi

Think about it ... you can't learn too much can you?

Our Gift To You!

Receive a free copy of Wallace D. Wattles book, "The Science of Getting Rich" with our compliments by sending an email to library@afabulousgroup.com - Just type FREE WATTLES BOOK in the subject line and we'll send it to you!

20

DEVELOP A MONEY MAGNET MINDSET

**"There is a secret psychology of money.
Most people don't know about it.
That's why most people never
become financially successful.
A lack of money is not the problem;
it is merely a symptom of what's
going on inside of you."**

T. Harv Eker

You may not realize it, but you actually have the power over your financial future. There are a number of things that you can do in order to attract the things that you want in life, such as money. Basically, you can develop a mindset that will help you to attract just about anything you want. When you think positively, you will be able to bring things into your world with ease. It's all about mindset.

Anyone who is negative all the time will end up falling into a pattern of negative energy, bad decisions and even a potential chain of destructive events. Instead of working on the negative things in your life and worrying or stressing out about everything, you can harness your energy and put it towards more positive thinking. Becoming a money magnet is something that you can do, however there are a number of people who do not realize just how easy it can be!

Becoming a money magnet means respecting money not wasting it. Start by appreciating what you do have. Be grateful and thankful for the things you have in your life currently. Then find ways to cut back on your spending and ways to save more. Being aware of your finances is a big part. Do you even know what your net worth is? If you don't know where you are, then how are you going to know where you want to go? Brainstorm new ideas and investigate opportunities to generate other sources of income, just open your mind and get creative.

You can also start by telling yourself each and every day that you are going to be successful. Wake up first thing in the morning, look into the mirror and state your dreams over and over again. These affirmations will help to start your day off in a positive manner. Many people who already take the time to speak repeated affirmations will tell you that they were the first step toward attracting the money that they wanted and deserved.

A good affirmation to use for this is simply, "I am a money magnet". Add that to your arsenal of affirmations and every time you receive, get or find money, even if it's just a penny, tell yourself out loud, "I am a money magnet". Remember your subconscious mind is like a genie and your wish is its command.

Did you realize that you can actually bring a world of success your way by surrounding yourself with others who are successful? If you know people in your life that you look up to, you are going to find that their positive energy will start to rub off onto you. Additionally, you will be able to find a number of tips and tricks from each of the people in your life that you can use in order to move forward with positive thinking and success.

You can do something such as keeping a journal or even putting together a vision board that you can look at daily in order to help you visualize and eventually attain your goals. If you dream it and believe it, you can become a money magnet. Soon, you will have the great cash flow coming in that you have always dreamt about.

"A big part of financial freedom is having your heart and mind free from worry about the what-ifs of life."

Suze Orman

Think about it ... people grow financially only as far as their minds will allow, expand your thinking and expand your wealth!

- 21 -

FIND A WAY TO GET PAID TO DO WHAT YOU LOVE TO DO

"If you want to achieve your dreams, you must follow them, and the best way to follow them is not to think about wanting to be very rich, but to think about doing something that you really want to do"

Jackie Collins

The last thing that you would want to do is find yourself stuck in a dead end job that seems to suck the life force out of you. All too often, people find themselves spinning their wheels in a certain career path just so that they can make ends meet. There must be something more. Something that you can do that you truly love, yet you do not know how to get yourself out of the rut and into a situation that is going to make you happy, pay the bills and at the same time achieve your financial goals.

When you are happy with your career and you are doing something that you truly love then you are going to excel at it. Some of the most successful people in the business world today have found themselves in their dream position. This is a position that they are excited to head off to every morning and they are thrilled to tell all of their friends and relatives about on a regular basis. You too can have a piece of that with a little bit of vision and effort on your part!

> **"Success is not the key to happiness.**
> **Happiness is the key to success.**
> **If you love what you are doing,**
> **you will be successful."**
>
> *Albert Schweitzer*

It might not always be as easy as picking up the paper, looking through the classified ad job postings and finding the position of your dreams. Sometimes, you have to put yourself on a certain career path that will eventually lead you to the vocation that you have always wanted. You might even find that you will need to do some volunteer work along the way to fill the happiness void until you can actually find a way to profit in your desired field. You may be surprised at how much joy and excitement this act of kindness will bring your way.

> **"If you're passionate about what it is you do,**
> **then you're going to be looking for everything you**
> **can to get better at it."**
>
> *Jack Canfield*

Ask yourself ... "What am I passionate about? What are some of my favorite hobbies or things to do? How could I make a living and achieve a level of financial security doing it? These three questions are the starting point to finding a way to a career you will love to do. Just let your subconscious mind and the universe start to work on the answers for you. Next, make a list of all the many avenues where you can make money doing them. Get creative here and brainstorm new ideas with others in your mastermind group. Pick the ones that feel right, that you feel most passionate about, trust your gut and pursue them diligently. Do all the necessary research, write out a plan to achieve it, take action and act as if you're already doing it.

Yes, there are always a number of curve balls that life can throw at you. If you have a career though that brings you joy and happiness, you are already winning half of the battle. Doing what you love that brings you a good income and a smile to your face will be something that can help you to overcome any number of obstacles.

"I'd rather be a failure at something I enjoy than be a success at something I hate."

George Burns

Think about it ... if you do what you love, you will never work another day in your life!

- 22 -

PAY YOURSELF FIRST / SAVE 10%

**"Compound interest is the eighth wonder of
the world and the most powerful thing
I have ever encountered."**

Albert Einstein

You may have heard the saying that if you pay yourself first you will save money. Do you understand the true meaning behind this theory? There are a number of people who forget to put themselves first whether it is in their personal life, business life, financial workings or even with their chosen career path. While it is always good practice to think of others, there is something to be said about taking care of yourself first before you can properly care for others and go on living your live as a happy and healthy being. So, take the time to pay yourself first. You may just find yourself saving 10% or more on all of your future endeavors!

You work hard for your money don't you? So, why do you give it all up to others first? Before you give your money to the government for taxes, the bank for your home and cars, the utility companies, pay yourself first.

A simple plan to start on your path to the financial freedom you desire is to pay yourself 10% of everything you make and create the habit of living on the other 90%. Then save and invest that money and use the miracle of compound interest to grow your money. With the right investment plan and compound interest, your money could end up making you more money than you could have earned working your entire life. This practice if continued over your lifetime will virtually guarantee financial success. Plus, it's easy to do if you have the right mindset and it will be hard to do if you have the wrong mindset. The choice is yours!

"Money isn't the most important thing in life, but it's reasonably close to oxygen on the 'gotta have it' scale."

Zig Ziglar

The simplest and painless way to do this is to set it up so it becomes automatic. Have the money taken directly out of your earnings either though a retirement account like a 401K or IRA, or use direct deposit. Just make this a habit, start now and start reaping immediate benefits.

"If you don't value money, you won't make the effort to control it. If you don't control it, you won't be able to save it. And if you don't save it, there won't be any surplus to invest."

Robert G. Allen

> ***Think about it*** *... if financial success is what you want to achieve in life then this needs to be a 'must' not a 'should', right? Right. So, start today!*

- 23 -

INVEST IN YOUR FUTURE

**"Buy when everyone else is selling and
hold until everyone else is buying.
That's not just a catchy slogan.
It's the very essence of successful investing."**

J. Paul Getty

A long time ago, you may have had a dream that one day you would have the financial freedom to do just about whatever you wanted. Today however, that dream of financial bliss may seem a little bit too far away to achieve. Instead of giving up on hope for a better financial outlook, it is in your best interest to look even further ahead and start investing in your future. After all, the one thing that you can hold onto in life is the hope for a better tomorrow. There is no time like the present to start investing in your future so that you can pave the way for great financial freedom or even wealth depending on your level of dedication.

"Rich people choose to get paid based on results. Poor people choose to get paid based on time."

T. Harv Eker

Investing in your future could be as simple as saving a couple of dollars away every day or each week when you get paid. While this investment may seem really small to you now, you are working towards the bigger picture. As you start to see your savings adding up, that money can then be invested in any number of platforms available today including the stock market, real estate, a new business and so on. With the wonder of compound interest you could get your money working for you and possibly make you more money than you could ever make working for a paycheck. When you get your money working for you, you're now working smarter not harder.

Next up, there is nothing greater than investing in yourself when you are thinking ahead to the future. While your health and well-being should always be in the forefront of your mind, you should know that as a human being you never stop learning. Start by reading a non-fiction self help book or autobiography of someone who inspires you. Success leaves clues, so learn from those before you. You could easily take 30 minutes per day, 15 minutes in the morning and 15 minutes before you go to bed to read. With just 30 minutes a day you could easily read at least a book a month. That's at minimum 12 books per year and 60 over 5 years. That investment in yourself alone will pay huge dividends in your future success.

Plus, with the vast number of ways that you can earn extra money today, especially on the internet, you are bound to find more than a couple of ways that you can invest in your future.

Your first step towards investing in your future should be developing a strong belief in yourself. After you believe in yourself and what you are capable of, the sky is the limit in terms of what you can achieve as well as the level of happiness that you can enjoy.

"There is nothing wrong in wanting to get rich. The desire for riches is really the desire for a richer, fuller, and more abundant life. And, that desire is praiseworthy."

Wallace D. Wattles

Think about it ... *it's your future and it starts today!*

- 24 -

SPEND LESS THAN YOU MAKE

"If you know how to spend less than you get, you have the philosopher's stone."

Benjamin Franklin

There are a great deal of people in the world who long to be rich. They seem to think that no matter what, having an excessive amount of money will help solve all of their problems. Some of the rich people that do have the money will say that along with the money comes a whole new set of problems that pop up in their lives.

One of the longest running financial secrets out there in the world today is that you can actually build and incredible amount of wealth simply by spending less money than you earn. It is really that simple? No matter what type of job you have or the kind of money that you make, if you are able to spend less than you bring home on a weekly, bi-weekly or monthly basis then you are going to see your finances building over time.

Wouldn't it be wonderful if money grew on trees? It is a nice thought, but one that is not realistic in any way, shape or form. What happens to be much more realistic is achieving the goal of living within your means. Certainly it is nice to have dreams of being able to spend wild amounts of money and there is nothing wrong with splurging on your self once in a while. Yet, taking your daily spending and putting a limit on it that you can stick to will help you to save an amazing amount of money that you can later invest for a return.

In order to be successful and have the things in life you really want you can't always be putting yourself deeper and deeper in debt. Have you ever looked around at people who seem to be able to live debt free? It is probably fair to say that these are people who practice the motto that you should always spend less than you earn. If you do not have the money to spend on an item or service, then you should try and wait until you do have the money. Putting added costs on your plate in terms of credit card debt can really hurt you financially over time. It is no secret that credit card interest rates and finance charges can keep you in a downward spiral of bills over the long term. Saving the money to actually pay cash for items and services is a great way to keep you debt free and on a budget.

> ## "Never spend your money before you have earned it."
>
> *Thomas Jefferson*

Depending on your career path, your finances can change for the better over time. However, with the number of life events that can come your way, it goes without saying that your financial future is never as "cut and dry" as you would like it to be. Spending less money than you earn on a consistent basis will help you to have a good financial safety net to fall back on should the need arise. All in all, this theory with the wrong mindset is a difficult one to follow, so adjust your mindset on saving and it will be one that will help you reap the most benefits throughout your life.

"Too many people spend money they haven't earned, to buy things they don't want, to impress people they don't like."

Will Rogers

__Think about it__ ... Jodi says, "for every dollar you don't spend it's really worth two ... the one you saved and the one you still have!"

- 25 -

NETWORK: DEVELOP YOUR MILLION-DOLLAR ROLODEX

"Your career, business, income and net worth will not increase until your contacts increase."

James Malinchak

It really goes without saying that you can find great success in your life based on the decisions that you make along with the type of people that you surround yourself with. Some of the most successful people in life are surrounded by a wealth of great people who they can count on should the need ever arise. Additionally, you would be amazed at the types of things that you can attain and learn when you happen to network, bringing all sorts of people into your world.

Networking has long been a way to associate yourself with a wide range of people, whether through business or on a social level. When you network, you are basically marketing yourself and putting your name and contact information out there so that you can associate with people who have similar interests and goals as you do. A critical aspect of networking is how you introduce yourself to others in a short period of time. It is imperative that you develop what has been called an elevator pitch, a 30-second presentation of you and what you do. From there you can build a 1 and 2 minute version to use in any social situation.

"Networking is an essential part of building wealth."

Armstrong Williams

With the popularity of the internet, there has been a whole new level of networking that has grown rapidly, almost taking on a new life of its own. While networking online, you can pretty much promote your business, enter into new business ventures, find people that you haven't talked with in a long time and so much more.

When you have a career or business that you have chosen, it is crucial that you network in order to find a great selection of people who you can lean on in order to advance further. As you start in on a career or business path, you are bound to make friends with a number of people in your chosen field. From there, you will be able to make more friends and business associates along the way. Down the line, the possibilities for additional business opportunities will be tremendous provided that you have filled up your Rolodex with all sorts of names and information of people throughout your lifetime.

When you look at all of the incredible social networking sites that are out there today like Facebook, Twitter, MySpace and LinkedIn to name a few, there is really a whole world of networking that is available to you. Many businesses are taking advantage of getting the word out about their websites,

89

promotions and much more all with the help of various social networking websites.

After you begin networking, you are going to see that a vast amount of opportunities will be opening up for you. When you talk to the right people then you can end up taking your life, business and career in a totally opposite and more rewarding direction than you had initially anticipated. There is nothing stopping you from making all of the proper connections that will boost you in the right direction. All you have to do is embrace all of the wonderful networking outlets that are available to you today and you will be well on your way to a fruitful Rolodex filled with information that can boost your career and business along with your social life.

> ### "It's all about people.
> ### It's about networking and being nice to
> ### people and not burning any bridges.
> ### Your book is going to impress,
> ### but in the end it is people that are
> ### going to hire you."
>
> *Mike Davidson*

Think about it ... it's not always what you know, but rather whom you know and who knows you that counts!

CREATE MANY SOURCES OF INCOME

**"I'm talking about residual income.
That's a fancy term for
a 'recurring' stream of income
that continues to flow
whether you're there or not"**

Robert G. Allen

Income gives you options, the more income you have the more options you have, but *residual income* offers you financial freedom. It is common knowledge that wealth can come in many different forms. Whether you are focused on your career or you are looking toward retirement, there are still ways that you can earn money and remain on top of your finances. The world today is literally chock full of wonderful ways that you can both earn an extra income as well as take the money that you already have earned and stretch your dollar even more. As you delve further and further into the world of online business or affiliate marketing, you can open up a whole new realm of making money.

In the way of numerous sources of income, there is nothing better than having your own home business. The great thing is that you can pretty much look at some of the things that you are passionate about and then build your own extra sources of income from there. Perhaps you have a full or part time job where you are happy and/or you make a decent amount of money. In addition to that job, you can look into one or more outlets to earn income from home.

A whole lot of people are working on websites that they maintain from home and sell everything from eBooks to products that they acquire via wholesale or even pieces that they crafted themselves. The sky is the limit once you decide to work from home with your very own online business. Basically speaking, if you can dream it then you can achieve it especially if you set your mind to it and work hard enough to reap the rewards.

Network Marketing or Multi-level Marketing (MLM) is another excellent source for additional income. You are already doing it now ever day of your life and you may not even realize it. So, why not get paid to do it? Every time you recommend something to someone, whether it be a movie, restaurant, beauty product, book, etc. that's simply network marketing. There are tons of network marketing companies out there, just find one where you love using their products or services, recommend it to others and get paid. If this additional source of income is of interest to you go to www.afabulousgroup.com for more information on various products we use and highly recommend.

"I'd rather have 1 percent of the efforts of 100 people than 100 percent of my own efforts."

J. Paul Getty

So, you never know just what life is going to throw your way. With the economy ever changing at any given time, it is a smart idea to have multiple sources of income that you can fall back on. People are finding more and more often that they are being laid off from their jobs or even having their hours cut back. When this is the case, you can work to supplement your income with whatever you have chosen as your work at home business.

You know that it is imperative that you form a solid web of security that will help you move forward in life. Not only do you want to have financial freedom, but it is also extremely important to have many sources of income so that you can use some of the funds should any type of crisis come your way. Here is a partial list of ideas for other extra streams of income you can develop:

- Write and sell a book or eBook
- Learn to trade the stock market
- Invest in Real Estate
- Sell on the internet
- Join a Network Marketing Company or MLM group
- Teach and/or speak on a topic as a leading authority
- Acquire a franchise doing something you're passionate about

**"I think it is a man's duty
to make all the money he can,
to keep all that he can, and
give away all that he can."**

John D Rockefeller

> ***Think about it*** *... it doesn't make sense to put all of your eggs in one basket, does it? Generate many sources of additional income to have the freedom you desire, and deserve!*

ACTION
STEPS
TO
SUCCESS

"If one advances confidently in the direction
of one's dreams, and endeavors to live the life
which one has imagined, one will meet with
a success unexpected in common hours."

Henry David Thoreau

- 27 -

SMILE MORE

**"A beautiful smile is a work of art,
a bright window to the soul, and a key instrument
to enjoying a fuller, richer life."**

Dr. Bill Dorfman

Smile, because when you smile you can't feel bad or sad and you make others feel glad. Try it, just smile.

There once was an old song that said 'If you're smiling, the whole world smiles at you'. If you think about it, these are really words that a person can live by. Even a person who is down on their luck can still get through the toughest of times as long as they still know how to put a smile on their face. There have even been a number of studies in the past to try to prove that a person can actually add a few years onto their life expectancy as long as they laugh and smile quite often throughout the course of every day.

**"Don't cry because it's over.
Smile because it happened."**

Dr. Seuss

For a long time now, people have been looking to positive thinking in order to help draw in the things that they would like out of life. If you go throughout life with a frown on your face then the chances are that you will end up drawing in all of the negative forces of nature that surround you. A smile is worth a thousand words, for sure. Additionally, a smile is also quite powerful when it comes to healing the sorrows of others around you who are in need of a positive light or a pick me up to their day.

"The only thing that warms the heart as much as a beautiful song is a beautiful smile."

Garth Brooks

When it comes to some of the ways that smiles can improve your life's path, all you have to do is think of stress and the negative effect it can have on you as well as the people around you. The more you smile, the more apt you are to cutting out daily stresses. When you eliminate a good amount of stress from your life, you are going to be able to better fight off various sicknesses. Your health and well being can actually be directly related to the number of smiles that you pass out to people around you each and every day.

Not only is a smile quite contagious, it (a smile) has also been known to be directly related to success. It should be quite easy to see that the people around you who are *"serial smilers"* are usually the ones who have good things going on in their lives. Besides, did you know it takes more muscles in the human body to frown than it does to smile? So, stop working so hard to wear that frown, it's easier to smile.

"A warm smile
is the universal language of kindness."

Unknown

A smile can also do wonders for your outward appearance. The majority of people in the world today are attracted to a good smile. If you are able to show your happiness or personality through a smile, then you are able to project your aura onto others. While a smile is surely not a cure for everything, one can certainly make just about anything a whole lot better.

"The reality in today's world is that a dazzling smile can ignite romance, increase your chances of career success, and boost self-confidence."

Dr. Bill Dorfman

Think about it ... look up to the sky and smile big. See, you can't feel bad when you smile and when you do it around others it makes them feel better too!

- 28 -

CREATE EMPOWERING HABITS

"Repetition of the same thought or physical action develops into a habit which, repeated frequently enough, becomes an automatic reflex."

Norman Vincent Peale

Your thoughts become words; your words become actions; your actions become habits and your habits form your destiny.

You know what you would like to do in life. You know what you should be doing in life. However, it is the road in front of us that often takes us on a winding path. In order to break the cycle and start on a path that gives you hope and meaning, then you need to become empowered from within. The wonderful thing is people of all backgrounds will find empowerment in many different ways.

After all, your habits, whether they are good or bad, can end up shaping the level of achievement that you will reach in your lifetime. In order to get the absolute best results, it is imperative that you get yourself on track with those good habits and put all of the benefits that you reap to good use.

"Chains of habit are too light to be felt until they are too heavy to be broken."

Warren Buffett

Washing away your bad habits may be easier than you think. The first step to eliminating old disempowering habits is awareness. Once a person starts to get into a certain comfort level within their life, it is all too easy to form a pattern. In order to break the cycle of your bad habits, you must first recognize what they are and figure out how you can work against them in a positive light. The most dominant habits that you have should be the ones that you work on first. Each of the habits that you change, one by one you are empowering yourself and allowing a path for good things to happen for you in the future.

Perhaps you have a habit that is negative in more ways than one. You may be a smoker or you might have the habit to procrastinate. Stomping out such bad habits should be replaced with one that is good and empowering. Once you do this, you are going to set yourself up for wonderful habits that can bring you joy and even financial gain in the future. The sky is the limit once you start to set your wheels of empowerment in motion.

Research shows that it takes 30 days to create a new pattern or habit. 30 consecutive days, which means if you miss one day you must start again at day 1. So do it and choose today to work on one new empowering habit and do it for 30 consecutive days and you will be amazed at how your life starts to change.

In life, there are no brick walls that you cannot face as long as you feel empowered. While it may be too difficult to knock down the wall, empowerment through empowering habits can help you to find ways to climb over or get around these brick walls.

**"Feeling sorry for yourself
and your present condition,
is not only a waste of energy,
but the worst habit
you could possibly have."**

Dale Carnegie

Think about it ... negative disempowering habits produce negative results, where as positive empowering habits produce desirable results!

- 29 -

SET SPECIFIC MEASURABLE GOALS

"A goal is a dream with a deadline."

Napoleon Hill

If you don't make a decision in life somebody will make them for you. That means you'll end up following someone else's path instead of your own. The best way to determine your future is to chart your own course. That's what setting specific measurable goals will do for you. You now will be the captain of your vessel sailing through life under your direction, not others.

Once you sit back to think about it, your entire life is actually riddled with unspoken goals. From the day that you were born you have a certain set of milestones that are placed in front of you that you are expected to not only reach, but to surpass. As you grow older, you can start to mold your own goals in a manner that will allow you to carve your own path throughout your journey in life. However, setting goals the right way and subsequently attaining them may be the portion that you have difficulty with along the way.

"A good goal is like a strenuous exercise - it makes you stretch."

Mary Kay Ash

A goal that is not specific with a definitive result and a day, date and time to accomplish is just a daydream or wish. When setting your goals be as detailed as you possible can and use all five senses. For example: What does your goal look like? How does it feel? What sounds are associated with it? Does it have a smell, aroma or taste? Just be as specific as you possible can when writing down your goals. Goals also need an exact date and time that you want to achieve them by. Now your subconscious mind has specific direction as to which it can start to process how to accomplish them.

Also, in order for you to achieve your goals you need to take massive action. Do something, even multiple things, each day whether the action seems large or small toward achieving your goals. A goal without action is a daydream. Besides, constant action eliminates procrastination.

Read your goals at least twice daily; ideal times are in the morning when you first wake up and at night just before you go to bed. This way you start your day on a positive note and at night you let your subconscious mind work on them. We've talked about habits, so make reading your goals a new empowering habit.

As a human being, you will find yourself dancing on a fine line between measurable goals and good intentions. While you feel as though there is a goal that will be easy to accomplish, you may constantly see that you will end up putting it off again and again. Measurable goals are a great way to experience little successes within your life. You never know the incredible feeling that these successes bring unless you create attainable and measurable goals. Plus, you set goals not so much to achieve the goal, but for the person you end up being because of the achievement of your goals.

Goal setting doesn't have to be difficult or a burden, so have fun with it. Remember this is your future you are laying out, if that doesn't excite you nothing will. With a big enough 'WHY' you can accomplish any goal.

"Goals give you more than a reason to get up in the morning; they are an incentive to keep you going all day. Goals tend to tap the deeper resources and draw the best out of life."

Harvey Mackay

Think about it ... it's your life, you have to live it, so don't you want to decide it for yourself?

For help with your goals and developing your 'WHY' please contact Jodi personally at coaches@SuccessCoachInstitute.com or visit www.SuccessCoachInstitute.com. Your first session is on us when you mention Millionaire Secrets In You. Contact us, you'll be glad you did!

- 30 -

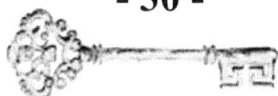

CREATE A VISION OF YOUR FUTURE: USE VISION BOARDS

"The best way to predict the future is to create it."

Peter Drucker

Looking ahead to the future may be something that you do on a daily basis. While there are all sorts of great ways that you can think of your future, you may want to find a good way to really visualize where you would like to be. After all, most personal development experts will tell you that when you are able to have a visual representation of something, you are better able to focus on it and help to reel that item or goal into your reality.

One of the best and most popular tools that many people are using today to help them plan their future and realize their dreams is the vision board. If you have never heard of a vision board, the chances are really good that you will want to start in on one right away. Now, you do not have to be extremely artistic or have a lot of money to spend on supplies in order to create a vision board. Just a little bit of thought, some good dreams and determination is all that you really need in order to create the perfect vision board.

A visual representation of any of your dreams can come in the shape of just about anything that sparks your imagination. If it has always been your dream to live in a particular house and area, you could cut out pictures of the house, landscaping, backyards, furniture, views of the area and other things you want in the house and tack them to your vision board. At the same time, somebody who wants to write a book can design a book cover with testimonials from celebrities to put on their vision board. Or, maybe you want a million dollars. You could find a picture of a $1,000,000 bill on www.GoogleImages.com or www.kevinklimowski.com for a free download of the one we use to glue to your vision board. Basically, if you can dream up something for your vision board and it gets you motivated, then you are on the right track!

The sky is the limit when you are creating your vision board and so should your dreams be as well. When you limit your dreams to what you think you may be able to achieve then you are actually robbing yourself from the chance to reach for the stars. You do realize that nobody ever became something special without raising the bar and working harder and harder each day until they attain their goals.

Perhaps there are certain words or quotes that really inspire you and get you motivated. These things are just right for your vision board and are sure to get your subconscious working each and every day. Make sure that you place your vision board in an area of your home or office where you will be able to see it often throughout the day. If you would like, you could even create more than one vision board depending on the number of dreams and goals that you have. Also, you can use your computer screen saver as a vision board as well.

If you would like to use the same vision board products and software programs we use go to www.SuccessCoachInstitute.com and click on resources (recommended products).

**"Look to the future,
because that is where
you'll spend the rest of your life."**

George Burns

Think about it ... if you don't design a vision of your future and a path to follow, someone will pick one for you. My guess is that you won't end up being very happy or excited about your future that way. Good luck!

- 31 -

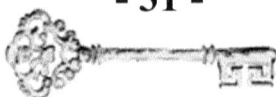

USE AFFIRMATIONS TO CONDITION YOUR SUBCONSCIOUS

"It's the repetition of affirmations that leads to belief. And once that belief becomes a deep conviction, things begin to happen."

Muhammad Ali

Affirmations are a powerful tool to recondition the conscious and subconscious minds and confirm to the universe a desired goal you want to achieve.

The power of affirmations can be quite incredible. If you repeatedly tell yourself something over and over again then slowly but surely your subconscious mind is going to catch up and take over. If you dream something over and over, can it really happen? Dreams can actually become reality and you can draw good things closer to you over time if you believe that it can happen. It is really that simple.

Life is a learning process. From the very moment that you are born, you are almost like a sponge. You soak up an incredible amount of information and your brain processes this information in a variety of ways. As you live your life as a child, you are told how you should act, what you should do in certain situations and hopefully you were properly taught right from wrong. With this being said, your family, teachers and the world around you are all of the factors that control your subconscious mind.

You must remember throughout your life from childhood until you became an adult that you were praised whenever you did something well or you met a certain milestone in your life. This praise then became the driving force that led you to move on and hammer out the next goal until you achieved success. One can almost look at positive affirmations as the same type of motivation. When you use affirmations as a constant daily reminder of what you want, what you can be and what you know you will be then you are pretty much guaranteed to be able to take yourself there with time.

Affirmations are a marvelous way to work constant positive energy into your mind. Because the mind is constantly working and firing, you have a greater chance of saturating it with this positive influence of affirmations. If you use affirmations properly, then you are going to see that they are incredible tools to have in your arsenal that you need in order to take on just about any situation that comes your way. When you think of the things that you want in your life and you repeatedly tell yourself about them or that you want to achieve, then things can start to fall in your favor.

Affirmations are definitely a whole lot more than simply words spoken in with a lot of repetition. If you are truly curious how affirmations can work or if you are open minded enough to try it, then there is no better time to get started than right now.

To download instructions on how to create positive and empowering affirmations that really work, visit our website at www.successcoachinstitute.com or send us an email requesting information on affirmations to info@successcoachinstitute.com.

**"You affect your subconscious mind
by verbal repetition."**

W. Clement Stone

Think about it ... *you become and have what you want, when you affirm it positively in your mind!*

- 32 -

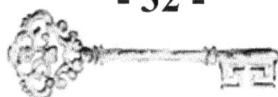

MEDITATION... RELAXATION... VISUALIZATION...

**"Visualize this thing that you want,
see it, feel it, believe in it.
Make your mental blue print,
and begin to build."**

Robert Collier

There are plenty of different things that you can try in order to realize some of your dreams. Of course, there is always good, old-fashioned hard work, however you need to make sure that you take care not to become too stressed or overworked. If you are like many people today, you are looking for a great way that you can realize your dreams in a way that will also help you to relax and minimize daily stress. When this is the case, you may want to look into a process that will include meditation, relaxation and visualization.

(More resources can be found at www.successcoachinstitute.com)

Throughout the course of time, healers and civilians alike have been using meditation as a way to work through any number of issues with the mind, body and soul. Whether you are suffering from an illness or looking for a way to relax when you come home from work, meditation can be a great way to get your body on track with your thoughts and more. However, did you realize that you can also use meditation and relaxation as a smart way to visualize your goals and put yourself on the right track for success?

"Hold a picture of yourself long and steady enough in your mind's eye, and you will be drawn toward it."

Napoleon Hill

For years now, this has been an incredible way to work with the subconscious mind in order to attain your goals. Basically speaking, just about anything that you desire in terms of mind, body and soul can be achieved with a proper regimen of meditation. The process can be as simple as starting with 15 minutes per day sitting in a quiet room by yourself with or without meditation music and just letting your body relax and your mind go free. Don't think or analyze your thoughts just observe and appreciate them. Over time you will find it easier and easier to achieve this state of relaxation through meditation and your sessions will become longer.

The key to success for the entire process is a combination of an open mind along with complete relaxation. Take a deep breath and relax so that you can fully focus on the task at hand. Think for a moment about just what it is that you are looking to achieve. Even though it may take you a few times in order to really see the results that you are looking for, many people who are already dealing with meditation, relaxation and visualization will tell you that the wait is well worth it.

Realizing what your dreams are and taking control of your life are two different things. In order to truly achieve success, you must fully focus on what it is you are going for and working at it until it happens. Meditation and relaxation is key when you are hoping to completely visualize and realize your goals in life. Once you achieve some or many of your goals, you could even be quite the inspiration for everyone else that surrounds you.

"Formulate and stamp indelibly on your mind a mental picture of yourself as succeeding. Hold this picture tenaciously. Never permit it to fade. Your mind will seek to develop the picture... Do not build up obstacles in your imagination."

Norman Vincent Peale

Think about it ... we can build so much stress through the course of daily activities that shut down our creative thinking. By meditating, relaxing and visualizing our goals we open our subconscious mind to its creative capacities!

- 33 -

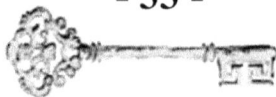

STOP PROCRASTINATING

"If you put off everything till you're sure of it, you'll never get anything done."

Norman Vincent Peale

It doesn't matter what level of success you have achieved in life, one of the biggest challenges we all face, at least from time to time, is procrastination. We know we need to do something, but we put it off for another time. The bottom line is that procrastination is a dream killer, time thief, and a bad habit.

The best and really only way to defeat procrastination is to take massive action now. Plan your work and work your plan. When you have something that needs to get done write out a plan with action steps and timelines and work the plan. This process keeps the mind focused and the timelines keep the urgency to do it now rather than put it off for another day.

Have you ever noticed two things when you procrastinate 1) You develop a certain level of stress, which can lead to all sorts of health problems, and 2) When you eventually get around to doing the thing you put off and finish it, you look back and think to yourself, 'why did I put off doing this?' For example, let's say you have been meaning to start an exercise routine for quite a while now, but you just keep putting it off. Then one day that 'should' now becomes a 'must' and you start. You make a conscious effort and now you've been exercising everyday for a week and you're starting to feel great. 30, 60 and 90 days go by and you feel incredible and you're in dynamic shape. At that point have you ever reflected back and asked yourself, *"If I only would have started this a year ago where would I be now?"* Procrastination is truly a thief of your time and time is perishable. We all have the same amount of it in a day so use it wisely and actively before it disappears.

What has procrastination cost you in terms of your finances and financial future? Every day you wait to start saving money in a retirement account or some other investment plan is costing you an outrageous amount of lost money in compound interest. What about all the lost revenue from the business you haven't opened yet, the website you've been meaning to create, the phone calls to prospects you haven't made or the book you've been putting off writing? What has procrastination now cost you in term of dollars and cents in your lifetime?

Many people use the excuse of not having all the information or it's not perfect yet. Stop with the excuses, nothing will ever be perfect, the time will never seem right and the best way to learn is as you go. Remember, its action that moves you forward, excuses only hold you back.

The simplest and easiest way to eliminate procrastination is to first be aware of when you're doing it. And two, make the choice to do it now not put it off. To do or not to do, the choice is yours.

You can also employ the support of your accountability partner or members of your mastermind to keep you focused and strong.

"Procrastination is the thief of time."

Joseph Heller

Think about it ... *why put something off for tomorrow, which you could easily do today?*

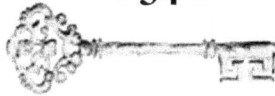

FAIL FORWARD FAST

**"For every failure,
there's an alternative course of action.
You just have to find it.
When you come to a roadblock, take a detour."**

Mary Kay Ash

Let's face it; if you are going to achieve anything in life you're going to have failures along the way. We all experience setbacks, obstacles, challenges, disappointments and even hardships on our journey though life. The good news is we can all learn something from each and every one of them. Every adversity carries with it a seed for a new opportunity to grow. Your job, if you will, is to never quit just because it didn't work out the way you expected the first time.

Failing is a part of life if you intend to get better at anything or achieve something amazing, so except it and prosper from them. Besides, failing is only failing if you assign it that way in your mind. Every successful person and inventor on Earth experienced some sort of setback, challenge, some level of failure in their pursuit of their goal. The difference has always been that the average person tends to get down, depressed, and loses interest. Inevitably quitting. No longer is this going to be you, you now will appreciate the situation, learn something from it and use it to forge on.

"Failure is success if we learn from it."

Malcolm Forbes

You always have a choice as to how you react and what meaning you give any event. When a challenge arises you will make a choice one way or another on how to treat it. You will fill your head with negative stuff that dis-empowers you, or you will accept it and make a choice to learn from it and push on.

A good way to face a difficult situation is to visualize yourself 5, 10 even 20 years from now having achieved all your goals. What would the future you tell the today you to do? How many times have you said to yourself, "If I only knew then what I know today?" Besides, once you get past the failures, you'll be surprised how easy getting though it actually was. Nothing is ever as bad as it first seems.

"The difference between average people and achieving people is their perception of and response to failure."

John C. Maxwell

***Think about it** ... you're going to fail and on the road to success and chances are good you're going to have setbacks, learn from them, don't give up and feel blessed because now you know one way it doesn't work!*

- 35 -

PRACTICE 'PERFECT PRACTICE'

"They say that nobody is perfect.
Then they tell you practice makes perfect.
I wish they'd make up their minds."

Winston Churchill

In today's demanding society, people are constantly striving to be the best that they can be. After all, in order to land the perfect job or get the things that you want in life, you have to be able to excel and take on the role of a go-getter. How do you get to the level where you would like to be? Anyone will tell you that it will take hard work, a lot of determination and loads of practice!

If you always do what you've done, you'll always get what you got. Any professional athlete, actor, celebrity, public speaker, etc. will tell you that to achieve an extremely high level of success you need to practice. Michael Jordan is considered by many to be the greatest basketball player of all time, Jerry Rice holds just about all the receiving records in the NFL, both men have been known to practice to improve their skills more than anyone else in their sports. And this holds true and consistent with any great success in any business or industry. You simply can't achieve a level of success without practice.

"My father taught me that the only way you can make good at anything is to practice, and then practice some more."

Pete Rose

Nobody ever wakes up knowing how to play classical music on the piano. Learning an instrument is just one example of how practice can get you further and further toward your desired result. In order to get to the success level that you would like, be it an instrument, sport, salesperson or speaker it is important to set goals for yourself and take the time to practice until you get better and better. While you are learning, it is imperative that you are able to take constructive criticism and feedback on how you are doing from your mentor and coaches or even your peers and clients.

There will be a number of things in your life where you will only attain greatness as long as you practice. Whether you are looking to master a sport, give an amazing presentation or be an outstanding salesperson, there is nothing better than buckling down and practicing.

Half of the battle in this lifetime will be realizing that nobody is perfect. While you may be able to achieve a perfect score on a test or you may find the perfect house to live in, there are many more things out there that will get better with a little bit of practice. If you look at your area of business, there is always room for improvement. Why would you want to be perfect anyhow? It would seem as though perfection would be a little bit boring and lonely. After all, when you are perfect, you have nothing left to strive for, right?

They always say that practice makes perfect, when in reality practice only makes you want to practice more and more. And it's not just practice, it's perfect practice that makes the difference. Simply logging time does not cut it. While it may seem to be a daunting task to practice something repeatedly, you must keep your eye on the prize at all times in order to keep things in perspective.

**"I know you've heard it a thousand times before.
But it's true – hard work pays off.
If you want to be good, you have to
practice, practice, practice.
If you don't love something, then don't do it."**

Ray Bradbury

Think about it ... *repetition is the mother of skill; it's the key to learning or improving on anything, so practice, perfect practice!*

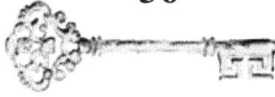

ACT AS IF

"One of the greatest strategies for success is to act as if you are already where you want to be."

Jack Canfield

If you want to be successful then act as if you are already successful. Start thinking and doing things successful people do and stop the thinking and actions of a poor person. Only by acting as if you can will you believe you can. The unconscious mind doesn't know the difference between fact or fiction, reality or imagination, so it will provide for you what you need to stay in that reality until you actually are there. By acting as if you start in motion the things you will need to make your current desires a reality.

One of the best things that you can do in your life is change your way of negative thinking into positive thinking. You know that you would like to act a certain way and that you have dreams of living a certain lifestyle. In order to get to this level within your life, you first must change the way that you think. While this may seem easy in the beginning, you have to keep yourself focused on the prize; otherwise you may end up falling into old routines.

You know that you would like things in your life and in your future, and then you must look forward instead of the way that things have been for you in the past. So what if you are making your way to a job interview that you are afraid you are not ready for? You need to project a strong outward appearance and show that you are incredibly confident in yourself and your ability and you will come out on top. Act as if you already have the job, and you will. And that holds true whether you're going for a business loan, finding a partner for a project, starting a new business, giving a speech, conducting a seminar, delivering a sales presentation or anything you want to have or do, just act as if.

"Whenever you do a thing,
act as if all the world were watching."

Thomas Jefferson

Also, never worry about what other people may think about you. If they are worth your time and they can appreciate you for the amazing person that you are, then they will be there for you. You will have the proper support system in place as long as you act as if you are worthy of it. Ask for help along the way and gather the support from the people in your life that care about you and want you to succeed. Negative thinking and negative people surrounding you will only work against you and bring you down.

You really cannot tell yourself no when you are trying to adopt the 'act as if' mentality. Since there is absolutely no room for negativity or the answer of 'no', then you need to learn how you can focus on the positive. Once you have positive thoughts and positive things going for you then great things are going to come your way. You would be amazed at the actions you can put in place in order to help you get the things that you desire and deserve in life.

Stay strong and act as if you have already won. If you stand strong and stick to your beliefs, setting aside any prior limits that you had set for yourself then you are going to do great things.

"You are not holding yourself back from success because you don't know 'how to succeed'. You are holding yourself back from success you are perfectly capable of, because you have more subconscious Why-Not-To's of Success than conscious Why-To's of Success."

Noah St. John

__Think about it__ ... if you believe you can do something, then by acting as if you already possess it and live in that vibration you will bring into your life that which you desire. That's simply living the "Law of Attraction"!

- 37 -

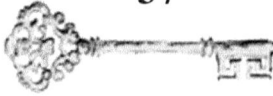

LIVE WITH INTEGRITY AND HONESTY

"No legacy is as rich as honesty."

William Shakespeare

Integrity defined is the adherence to moral and ethical principles, soundness of moral character. Honesty defined is the quality of being honest; uprightness and fair; truthfulness, sincere and free from deceit or fraud. These are two very critical traits of a quality person and living a life that is filled with honesty and integrity may be much harder than one would think. You must first embrace the qualities and make a decision to live by them.

As you go throughout your life, there are many obstacles that will come your way and the manner in which you deal with them will have a great deal of impact on your level of integrity. Of course, you can go through life cutting corners in order to get ahead or even tell a couple of white lies when you feel as though you have the need. However, are you really doing yourself any favors by having this type of outlook on life?

If you had any solid background while you were growing up, then you probably learned the major differences between wrong and right. However, there are many people that dance on the edge of doing what is right and what is convenient to them at the time. In order to truly live a life that is filled with integrity and honesty you have to remember to treat others surrounding you in a manner in which you would expect to be treated. This idea can apply to both your personal and professional life and as a matter of fact, both your personal and professional life are related in a sense when you are speaking of integrity and honesty.

"Integrity is the essence of everything successful."

R. Buckminster Fuller

When you look at how you want to live your life, you will surely see that there are a number of ways that you can take on the situations that come your way. Think of some of the factors that mold you into the person who you are and the person who you would like to become. Do you have trust? A trust in yourself and what you can achieve is definitely important. At the same time, if others have trust in you then you are going to see many more doors opening for you when it comes to potential opportunities that are going to boost your finances.

"One of the most important ways to manifest integrity is to be loyal to those who are not present. In doing so, we build the trust of those who are present."

Steven R. Covey

Take pride in what you do. When you have a strong sense of pride in the way that people think of you along with the characteristics that you posses then you will see your reputation growing exponentially. The last thing you will want is to see your reputation suffering any sort of blow that will make your friends, family or colleagues think any less of you. Taking great pride in yourself as a person as well as all of the accomplishments in your life will help to mold you into a person that oozes integrity.

Always be sure to care for each and every relationship within your life. You can almost use the comparison of relationships to plants or flowers in that you have to nurture them in order for them to grow. Once your good relationships grow, you will be able to later reap the benefits. Sure, it is easy to say that you are an honest person with integrity that others can look up to. However, those are simply words if your actions do not fall in line.

> **"As we express our gratitude,**
> **we must never forget that the highest appreciation**
> **is not to utter words, but to live by them."**
>
> *John F. Kennedy*

> ***Think about it ...*** *people associate with the people they know, like and trust. When you live in integrity and honesty more and more people will want to be around you, partner and do business with you. Your success is complimented by being successful!*

BE GRATEFUL AND APPRECIATIVE

**"Develop an attitude of gratitude,
and give thanks for everything that happens to you,
knowing that every step forward is a step toward
achieving something bigger and better than your
current situation."**

Brian Tracy

Be grateful and appreciative for what you have in life and never take anything for granted.

Do you remember sitting around the dinner table talking about all of the things you were grateful for? Well, as life goes on the chances are pretty good that you will start to lose sight of the things in life that you should remain appreciative of. Sure, you are happy that you have friends or family, or that you have a career and good health. But, are you really and truly grateful for all of the little things in life? You just may be one of the people that tend to take way too many things for granted. Perhaps it is time that you take a look back at your life in order to find out what you should truly be grateful for.

Once you do sit down and reflect on the various aspects of your life, you may find that there are hundreds of even thousands of things that make you happy. Being thankful for each and every one of these little things in life can really make you a more successful person in the long run. As a matter of fact, you might want to take and jot down the many things that you are thankful for. Develop a daily habit of writing down what you are grateful for and appreciate each day in a journal. Just so when a rough patch hits you can look back and remember what you have to live for and look towards in your life.

"A simple grateful thought turned heavenwards is the most perfect prayer."

Doris Lessing

Simply knowing that you are alive is a major reason to be grateful. Life is short and it can all be taken away from you within the blink of an eye. I know I had a life-changing event happen to me. Living to see another day is something that many people really take for granted. All you have to do is look at a family who lost a loved one due to a car accident or a sudden illness and you will see true pain and loss. Knowing that the sun is rising on you for one more day should be plenty to make you look at the brighter side of every gloomy situation that comes you way.

With an economy that can change at any moment, if you have a career that brings you an income that supports you and your family, that is yet another huge reason to be grateful and appreciative. It is extremely unfortunate, but there are a large number of families that are torn apart from the loss of a job and then the turmoil that can follow. By the same token, say that you are one of the unfortunate who does suffer the loss of a job. The simple fact that you are living for another day to find another career to keep on going is a blessing in its own right.

While it may sound silly, you can also be grateful for the difficulties and stresses that you may encounter in your lifetime. Reflect for a minute. If you didn't have issues or situations arise that call for your attention, you are going to miss out on the stuff that helps to build your character. When you have the amazing ability to work through your problems, then you are going to develop a tremendous amount of strength that can and will trickle down to every other aspect of your life.

> **"Choosing to be positive and having a grateful attitude is going to determine how you're going to live your life."**
>
> *Joel Olsteen*

> ***Think about it ...*** *success is an opinion and when you live with an attitude of gratitude and you truly appreciate and are grateful for what you have, that's a pretty successful life, wouldn't you agree?*

- 39 -

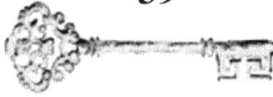

RESPECT OTHERS AND THEIR TIME

**"I've learned that people will forget what you said,
people will forget what you did,
but will never forget how you made them feel."**

Maya Angelou

You remember the "Golden Rule" ... *"The one with the gold makes the rules."* No, just kidding ... a little joke there. The real "Golden Rule" states, "Do onto others as you would have them do unto you." That means, treat others as you would like them to treat you. When it comes to others around you, it is imperative that you respect them and the time that they have to work with.

As a society, we have fallen into an endless cycle where we are constantly putting ourselves on a schedule or trying to beat the clock. There are so many things that you want to get done, however there are only so many hours within each day where you can reach your goal. When it comes to others around you, it is imperative that you respect them and the time that they have to work with. After all, your schedule is not the same as everyone else's and it is important that you look for ways to work around time issues that will be able to benefit everyone.

But, how can respecting others and their time contribute to the level of success you want to achieve? Keep in mind that success is a team sport and you will many times need the help of others to accomplish a goal or project. If you always are treating people with respect including their time, people will be more than thrilled to lend a hand. There is nothing a busy mover and shaker hates then someone to waste their time. Awareness is the best way to remember to respect others.

"Our attitude toward others determines their attitude towards us."

Earl Nightingale

Stop for a moment and give some thought to how often you find yourself procrastinating when you should be doing something else. Perhaps you are working on a project with someone or for someone, but you have a strong lack of motivation or inspiration that is holding you back. You have to think about the person who is waiting for you to finish whatever it is that you are working on. They probably have a schedule as well and they are depending on you to get finished in a timely manner. A deadline is a deadline and you have to respect yourself as well as others and their time.

In business if you set an appointment with someone be on time, don't be late. Being late only upsets the other person, but it also throws off their entire schedule. Also, it will make it extremely difficult to win back that persons respect and prolong or even eliminate any chance of doing business with them. If an emergency does arise or for some reason you can't make the appointment be courteous enough to call the person and let them know you will be unable to make it and need to reschedule. They will appreciate it and the relationship will remain strong.

Respecting others also means not picking on or making fun of others. Nobody respects a person who gossips or talks about someone behind their back. If you have a challenge or troubling situation with someone talking about it to someone else who can't do anything about it won't help the outcome. It is always best to show the person some respect and approach them individually to discuss the problem. No matter what the result they will respect you for keeping it between the two of you.

Plus, keep your promises and commitments, the quickest way to lose the respect of others is to renege on promises and break commitments. Your attitude and the way you think about and treat others will most certainly be a factor in you achieving success in your life. Again, life is a team sport and you can't do it alone, but if you don't respect others and their time eventually nobody is going to want to play on your team.

"Think first-class about everyone around you and you'll receive first-class results in return."

David J. Schwartz, PH.D.

Think about it *... if you treat and respect people the way you want to be treated and respected, they will be happy to reciprocate!*

- 40 -

MANAGE YOUR TIME,
DON'T LET YOUR TIME MANAGE YOU

**"Don't be a time manager, be a priority manager.
Cut your major goals into bite-sized pieces.
Each small priority or requirement
on the way to ultimate goal
becomes a mini goal in itself."**

Denis Waitley

What is the one thing every human being on this planet runs out of everyday of their lives? **Time**. Don't waste yours.

Time is truly one of those things that you have to learn how to manage otherwise you are going to go crazy. Unfortunately, too many people fall into the trap of letting time manage their life instead of the other way around. In order to have a good solid schedule where you still have free time to enjoy, you really have to learn how to manage your time and not let time manage you.

"Either you run your day or your day runs you."

Jim Rohn

Many people run around all day long from one task to the next, often times in a scatter-brained state trying to accomplish things that need to be done. Some people are so busy with their careers that they have no time to relax, unwind or enjoy their families. Others sit around watching TV wasting time when they could be reading, meditating or taking action on a goal, if they even have goals. Successful people always find a way to better manage their time.

Of course, life is full of surprises and you truly never know what is waiting for you around the next corner. Because life is uncertain, it can be almost impossible to plan out each and every second of your day. If you stop to think about it, would you even want to have every minute of the day planned out for you? After all, there is something wonderful and exciting about being able to do something at the drop of a hat. The people in life that are truly happy are the ones that know how to manage their time in a manner that allows plenty of pleasure and business and never stresses about the little things.

"Time equals life; therefore,
waste your time and waste of your life,
or master your time and master your life."

Alan Lakein

One of the best ways to manage your time is to prioritize your schedule. We learned a great system from America's #1 Success

Coach, Jack Canfield, my coach and mentor, and have included our version here.

Prioritize you schedule by planning out 3 specific types of days (productivity, flex and free/fun) in your week, month and year as:

> The first are **productivity days**; these are the days you focus 100% of your time on the things that derive 80% of your income or companies revenue. On these days you keep side conversations to a minimum, TV's off, phones can be off as well and you don't read unproductive emails, you do what needs to be done.

> The second days are **flex days**; these are the days you use for errands like dry cleaning, banking, checking emails, returning phone calls and tying up loose ends. You use these days to finish up any incompletes in your life.

> The third days are **free or fun days**; no working on these days whether its business or personal. You simply do what you want to have fun; go on a vacation, spend time playing with the kids, go to a movie, watch TV, play golf or go fishing, it doesn't matter just have fun and relax. Remember on fun and free days no business calls or emails. Now in your business you may need to train your colleagues on how to handle things themselves on these days. But, if you surrounded yourself with a solid reliable team this should never be a challenge.

Your life is what you make of it and if you would like to see your time managed more wisely, you must put a system in place immediately that works for you.

**"Don't be fooled by the calendar.
There are only as many days
in the year as you make use of.
One man gets only a week's value out of a year
while another man gets a full year's
value out of a week."**

Charles Richards

> ***Think about it*** *... make sure what you do today is important because you are trading a day of your life to invest in your future!*

- 41 -

LET GO AND DELEGATE

"You can delegate authority, but not responsibility."

Stephen W. Comiskey

Sometimes, it can be difficult to let go of the reigns of a project or task in order to let somebody else help you out. While you may know that it is in your best interest to let go, it sounds a lot easier to do than it actually is. However, when you find yourself in a busy and stressful situation, you might even find that your project or job will end up suffering if you are completely unable to let go and delegate. All too often, people take on a whole lot more than they can handle, whether it is in your career or at home. Maybe it is time that you look at letting go of some of your burden by delegating in order to give yourself a much needed break.

You're not Superman or Superwoman so please stop trying to be. You can't do and be all things to all people. There are activities you excel at and some you struggle with. There are tasks that when you do them move you forward and produce revenue and tasks that need to be done but are time wasters and aren't very revenue generating. So, delegate the stuff in your life you're not good at or take up time that could be spent on more productive activities. Now you free up your schedule to do more of what will produce the results you want and achieve the goal you set.

It really does not matter if you are in a personal setting or a professional one. There are always things that we can delegate to others for them to do in order to help out. When in your business, delegating is a great way to help get a project done. At home take the time to delegate some chores and light tasks to some of your family members or friends so that you can ease your burden.

Your time is valuable, and there are things in life that need to be done, so don't waste precious time. When delegating make sure to factor in your time value, let's say you figure your time to be valued at $50 per hour. Then doesn't it make sense to hire someone to do a job like house cleaning, yard work or research for a book or project at $10 per hour and use that time to work on what earns you $50 per hour?

Now let's take it up a notch and think big with a millionaire's mindset. When delegating consider the "521 Rule" which states that $521.^{00} per hour is the minimum wage to be a millionaire (working 40 hours per week for 48 weeks per year). So having a millionaire's mindset means to start delegating all tasks that earn you less than $521.^{00} per hour and only focus on the activities that produce $521.^{00} per hour or more in returns for your business.

As you think of how you can delegate for any given situation, it is important that you take into consideration the skills and experiences of all of the people who you plan on using to spread out some of the work load. Remember that as you delegate, you are putting people on certain tasks, not looking for individuals to take care of your responsibilities for you. To be successful you need to let go and delegate.

**"Executive ability is deciding quickly
and getting somebody else to do the work."**

Earl Nightingale

> ***Think about it ...*** *when delegating use the 80/20 rule; figure out what you do that produces 80% of your income or desired outcomes, then you do those things and delegate the rest!*

- 42 -

SAY 'PLEASE' & 'THANK YOU!'

"God gave you a gift of 86,400 seconds today. Have you used one to say 'thank you'?"

William Arthur Ward

Why is it that you need to say please and thank you? Shouldn't simply asking for what you want be enough? Well, you can go through life without saying thank you for the goods or services that you are given, but you will never benefit from this. If you step back and look at your life, there should be many things that you can be thankful and grateful for. There are hundreds if not thousands of little things that many people take for granted. Being thankful and appreciative for all of these things will help you to build character as well as realize the importance of day to day gifts.

You should have been taught at a very early age that it is appropriate to say *"thank you"* in addition to *"please"* and other niceties. Not only are these common courtesies, but these few simple words can have a great impact on your life. In just about any situation that is going negatively, kind words such as thank you can generally turn the situation around. At the same time, saying please is a nice way to let someone know that you need help. All too often, people tend to forget that it is important to phrase their feelings properly.

There should never be any time in your life that you just take and take and take. Giving back to others is a wonderful thing that should not only make you feel good about yourself but also lend to amazing karma building up in your corner. In fact, how do you react when you give to another person and they do not thank you? The chances are very good that this is not something that you enjoy feeling. After all, when you work hard to help someone or give of yourself, a thank you is a free form of paying back.

When it comes to life in the business world studies show that the most asked for incentive to motivate people to do a better job is the gift of appreciation. A simple please when asked to do something and then thank you when they finish is sometimes all ones needs to feel appreciated. So, if you need help from a co-worker or colleague, then you can simply ask for help, however remember to say please! Then, once they follow through with help on their end, a thank you is certainly in order. After you seal the deal with a thank you, then you are opening up the door for more business transactions in the future that is the 'law of attraction'.

There are many things in life that you can tend to forget as you get busy or caught up in daily projects. If somebody helps you out in any way, shape or form, then a thank you of some sort is in order. Saying *"please"* and *"thank you"* aren't hard to do … you simply need to be **aware** to do it.

**"If the only prayer
you ever say in your entire life
is 'thank you',
it will be enough."**

Meister Eckhart

Think about it ... *for success to
come your way live with an
attitude of gratitude!*

- 43 -

HANG OUT WITH PEOPLE
YOU'D MOST LIKE TO BE LIKE

**"Be careful the environment you choose for it will
shape you; be careful the friends you choose
for you will become like them."**

W. Clement Stone

People who tell you that you can't do something are like a
pebble in your shoe. Do you let the pebble stop you? No. You
get rid of it and just keep going. You need to get away from or
completely eliminate the negative, de-motivating and pessimistic
people in your life. Why? Because in life you become like whom
you hang out with most often. You become a product of your
environment. The quickest, simplest and easiest way to become
successful is to hang out with successful, self-motivating, and
empowering people. You want to make more money, then hang
out with people that make the kind of money you want. After
time spent with them you'll start finding yourself thinking,
talking and acting just like they do. You'll start doing the same
things they do to make money, make the same kind of
investments they do, read the same books as them, even shop at
the same stores and eat at the same restaurants.

Whether you want to realize it or not, the people that you surround yourself with can have an incredible impact on your actions as well as your thoughts. If you are focusing your time and attention on people who are not motivated or goal oriented, then the chances are very good that you will become the same unmotivated individual over time. Simply make note of the 10 people you spend most of your time around. Take their salaries or income levels, add them up and divide by 10. My guess is that your salary or income level is somewhere close to that average. Why is this? Again it's because you become like those you hang around with the majority of the time.

"Motivation is simple.
You eliminate those who are not motivated."

Lou Holtz

When you want something, you should be surrounding yourself with people who either want the same things or better and are equally as successful as you would like to be. The more positive influence you have around you, the better chance you will have of striving to do better for yourself. After all, your life is not going to change for you. It is important that you draw on positive energy and surround yourself with people who you would like to be most like. In the end, they can be the driving factor that brings you to the success that you would like to achieve.

Surrounding yourself with individuals that you respect and look up to will draw nothing but wonderful things your way. When you have a dream, there are people out there who will talk you down and others who will lift you up. Wouldn't you rather choose the latter? It is impossible to succeed if you are around people who are not great influences or are supportive in any way. You are sure to see success will come easier then you think as long as you have people in your life to mirror and look up to.

**"When people are like each other
they tend to like each other."**

Anthony Robbins

> ***Think about it ...*** *if you truly want to soar with the eagles then you can't continue to flock with the turkeys!*

- 44 -

ASK FOR HELP

"Asking is the beginning of receiving. Make sure you don't go to the ocean with a teaspoon. At least take a bucket so the kids won't laugh at you."

Jim Rohn

No matter how smart or competent you are there will be times in your life when you can't do everything by yourself. It is these times that you will need to ask for help. Just know that it's okay to ask for help. You can't be all things all the time. Plus, some things simply aren't worth your valuable time to be doing yourself. There are others who can and will be able to do the task or chore quicker, easier and more efficiently than you, you just need to ask for help.

Asking for help is all about leveraging your time and talents. It's knowing that it doesn't serve you best to do it yourself. Many people feel a sense that they have to do it all, basically they're control freaks. They don't think that others can do it better than them, so they struggle to ask for help. If you're like this you need to relax and let go in order to achieve success. Again, success is a team sport and there is no 'I' in team.

Asking for help doesn't mean you're weak or incapable, it means you're aware of whom you are and you know what you need to do and what you can let others do to be more efficient.

Do you have a task or project that needs to be complete, yet you feel overwhelmed while trying to take it on by yourself? This is where it becomes imperative that you learn the importance of asking for help should the need arise. There is nothing wrong with admitting that you could benefit from an extra perspective or another set of hands to help you achieve your goals.

When asking for help on anything, for it to be done to your to satisfaction you need to communicate the details clearly and completely. Don't just assume that the other person knows what it is you're expecting. By taking the time to go over all the requirements you will speed up the process and make sure it gets done properly the first time. This will allow you to stay focused on the part of the project or task you are responsible for.

Learning to ask can also be very beneficial in your personal affairs as well. By simply starting to ask for things you could find yourself possibly getting free upgrades on hotels and car rentals, discounts on retail purchases, reduced credit card rates, lower interest rates on loans and lots of other free stuff. The money you save can then be invested to help you achieve your goals for financial independence. No amount is too small and every penny starts to add up. When you show the universe you respect money it will start giving you more to handle.

**"People who ask confidently
get more than those who are
hesitant and uncertain.
When you've figured out
what you want to ask for,
do it with certainty,
boldness and confidence."**

Jack Canfield

Think about it ... when you ask you get. The more you ask the more you get. You don't ask, you don't get!

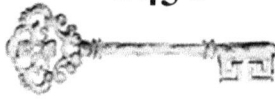

GATHER A GOOD TEAM: MENTORS, COACHES AND ACCOUNTABILITY PARTNER(S)

"A personal coach can help you discover what you truly want to do-and can help you determine the steps and the actions necessary to get there."

Jack Canfield

Often times, it can be easy to get caught up in the notion of what you think you need to do instead of looking right in front of you for what will work best. In order to gather information on what will suit you best, you should think about putting a great support system in place or rally together a team of people who can really work with you in order to help you realize and attain all of your dreams and goals in life.

Have you ever given much thought about having a mentor in your life that you can look to for answers? How about a coach? Many successful people today are enlisting the help of a life coach in order to help them get organized and remain focused on the prize. What about an accountability partner? The chances are pretty good that you may not even know exactly what any of these people really can do for you in terms of your life and well-being.

"Mentoring is a brain to pick, an ear to listen, and a push in the right direction."

John C. Crosby

A mentor is someone that has been there, done that, and can help you avoid some pitfalls while accelerating your learning though their experiences. A coach can help you overcome your weaknesses and build on your strengths. They know who you are and what you're capable of doing and push you to get better and better. An accountability partner is that person that holds you accountable for what you say you're going to do and vice versa. They can also be a tremendous support system to keep you motivated and moving forward when things get tough or obstacles pop up in your way.

Basically speaking, these three support systems are all very similar. No matter how you slice it, a mentor, a coach and an accountability partner are all people who are there to work with you and your life. Your life plan is an important piece of your happiness puzzle. You want to make sure that you have a life plan in place that suits you, that you execute it properly and that you have somebody that will be there in order to help you remain focused all the way through.

"A life coach does for the rest of your life what a personal trainer does for your health and fitness."

Elaine MacDonald

Perhaps you have always wanted to get to the gym and work out so that you can stay on track with your health and well being. You might go to the gym on occasion, yet you have a hard time remaining focused or sticking to the proper plan. A personal trainer can fall into line as a member of your life team that can help you attain your important fitness goals. With a personal trainer, you can tone up and lose 20 pounds if you would like. Without a personal trainer on your team, you may lose 5 pounds at best and slack on the proper diet to boot!

The same is true in any aspect of your life whether it be finances, a new business and your desired level of success. A good team that you can learn from, grow and keep you motivated is priceless. I'll tell you what; you probably won't be as successful as you deserve to be without them.

But, do you have to spend all kinds of money for a mentor, coach or accountability partner? Of course not! A coach is probably more affordable than you think. If you desire greater results in your life or simply want to get unstuck a coach can help you accomplish that. I invite you to go to www.successcoachinstitute.com, and click on the coaching link to read about the coaching program we have to offer. With the right coach you can really accelerate your progress towards success. As a matter of fact, you may find that you already have these people within your current network of friends, family members or colleagues. You simply have to find which of these people can be there for you and help you remain focused and motivated.

The new you is in there, just waiting to get out. When you make the time to gather a dream team of support, then you are going to see great things coming your way through hard work, determination and an incredible amount of motivation on your part!

**"Study anyone who's great, and
you'll find that they apprenticed to a master,
or several masters.
Therefore, if you want to achieve greatness,
renown, and superlative success,
you must apprentice to a master."**

Robert G. Allen

Think about it ... there is no "I" in team. So, put together a team that has the experience plus knowledge and one that wants to see you become all you can be!

- 46 -

JOIN OR START
A MASTERMIND GROUP

"When a group of individual brains are coordinated and function in harmony, the increased energy created through that alliance becomes available to every individual brain in the group."

Napoleon Hill

As a human being, you should be constantly looking for people or groups of people who you can look to in order to grow and bounce ideas off of in various ways. One way to do this is by putting together what is called a mastermind group in order to work through ideas and achieve great things. The most successful people since the early twentieth century through present day participated in mastermind groups. People like Henry Ford, Andrew Carnegie and Thomas Edison for example all shared in a mastermind. Perhaps it is time that you found out what a mastermind group is and how you can join or start one.

Basically speaking, a mastermind group is essentially just like the study group that you may have enjoyed back in high school or college. However, these are a gathering of people that can work together to attain the success that each and every one of them longs for in life. You can start a mastermind group filled with individuals who have a wide variety of knowledge and skills to bring the ideas that you all have into fruition.

Masterminding is a fabulous way for people to get support and new ideas from other liked minded individuals. The size of your mastermind group can vary, but its common practice to have four to six in the group. Anymore than that and not everybody may get their needs met and any less you might not get enough good ideas or insights to help your cause.

The process of a mastermind group is pretty straight forward. Although the group can pick the length, time and frequency of the meetings, what seems to work ideally is once a month or every other week on the phone for about an hour. That should be ample time for each member of the group to get 8 – 10 minutes to voice any challenges they are having or questions they need answered, plus hear the responses from the group. Pick one person to be the time keeper so the meeting flows smoothly and everybody gets their full time and you're good to go.

When you decide to put together a mastermind group, be sure that everyone that you bring in is on board with what your idea or goal is. By ensuring that you have people with you that are just as focused and determined as you are, then you are going to see incredible results fast. Also, it is extremely important that you have some level of a trust and ability to work with each and every one of the people who you choose for your mastermind group. Having people together that are constantly butting heads will do nothing except cause a lot of frustration for everyone involved.

There are two schools of thought when forming a group and neither is actually better than the other. The first thought is a group filled with people who have the same interests or careers. This way you can share what's working or not working in your industry. The second thought is a group filled with people from different but complimenting fields of expertise. This way you can get several different perspective and possible joint ventures.

When picking members for your group, remember you want to be around like minded people that lift you up, not bring you down. Try to choose people who have a higher level of success than you, so you can learn and grow.

"For when two or three are gathered together in my name, then am I in the midst of them."

Matthew 18:20

Think about it ... if two heads are better than one, having four or five working in harmony should be amazing!

- 47 -

BRAINSTORM NEW IDEAS

"Ideas are the beginning points of all fortunes."

Napoleon Hill

Do you think that some of the top inventors in the world were able to develop new products without tossing ideas back and forth with the people around them? Of course not! Even the greatest mind will benefit tremendously from the sharing of thoughts and ideas with others. This process is one that we know as brainstorming and it has been an incredible source of good thoughts and ideas for many, many years now.

The human mind grows stronger and stronger the more that you work it and the process of brainstorming can strengthen the mind, drawing out creativity and bringing forth incredible ideas. When you are able to be creative and share that thought process with others, the possibilities are endless. The brain itself is capable of truly amazing things, so it is easy to see why magic can happen when you put two or more minds together to work on a new ideas.

When you are at work, you may find that you have a number of issues that will arise over the course of time. Instead of working by yourself and taking on a tremendous burden, you may want to see if you can brainstorm with some of your colleagues in order to come up with new ideas or resolutions. You can work together as a team to help overcome any obstacles that are in your path. Before you know it, your brainstorming session could quite possibly be one of the biggest breakthroughs that you have had for your company.

Ideas may pop in your head while you are eating breakfast in the morning, working out at the gym, even in the shower or car. Take the time to jot some of these ideas down on a note pad that you carry along with you or record them with a pocket size recorder. How many times have you had an idea for something only to forget it a short time later? Studies show that short term memory lasts about 40 seconds, so record all ideas for further discussion and evaluation later.

Keeping your brain healthy in order to form great, new ideas actually takes some effort on your part. The best way to promote brain health is to take care of you first. The chances are pretty good that if you are not eating right, getting enough rest or even exercising like you should be then you are not going to be able to use your mind as the creative force that it has the potential of being.

Brainstorming is a truly amazing way to accomplish just about anything. Whether you are working on project at the office or you are looking to put together a volunteer program that will benefit one of your favorite charities, brainstorming can help you realize your dreams. Bouncing ideas back and forth off of another person is nothing new; just make sure that you are not afraid to express your thoughts and ideas openly!

"A man may die, nations may rise and fall, but an idea lives on."

John F. Kennedy

Think about it ... the seed to all great inventions stemmed from an idea!

ASK FOR FEEDBACK AND LISTEN TO IT

"There is no failure, only feedback."

Robert Allen

While it may be difficult to digest at times, feedback is one of the things in life that helps you to mold yourself into an individual. On a personal level, positive or negative feedback can help you with any of your friendships or relationships even when it involves your family. When it comes to a professional level, any type of feedback that you receive and listen to will help you to better yourself and your career. However, the real problem lies in actually asking for feedback when it is necessary and then listening to it no matter how difficult it may be to do.

Look at feedback as a smart tool to help you in many different ways because it's not there to harm you. While you may just think of feedback as a type of opinion, this information can work in your favor. All you have to do is use the feedback to your advantage whether it is good or bad. Often times however, you may find yourself hearing feedback that is not necessarily what you would expect or even want to hear at the time. You need to take a moment to look at the reasoning for the feedback and then analyze whether or not it is going to be able to help you in the future.

A great way to ask for feedback is to use the question; "On a scale of 1 to 10 with 10 being the highest, how would you rate 'whatever it is'? Then whatever the number is (except if it's a 10) ask the follow up question; "What would it take for it to be a 9 or 10?" These two questions will work in any situation where you want feedback so you can improve.

Where people tend to go wrong is when they fall into a thought process that the feedback is *actually* just a criticism of something they are saying or doing. Once you build up a wall of thinking that you are constantly being criticized, then you are never going to be able to take the feedback for what it is … things that you can use it to your advantage. Knowing that positive or even negative feedback is not a dig at you professionally or personally can help open you up to receive it. When you close yourself off to positive or negative feedback, then you are closing yourself off to valuable information that can be used in a number of ways.

Asking for feedback can be a whole different story entirely. While people always have opinions that they are dying to throw at you, it can make you quite humble if you have to ask for feedback. On a professional level, asking for feedback does not mean that you are less proficient or unqualified in your career. Asking for feedback in your business simply means that you are looking to solidify your thought process or get a second opinion on a project in order to do everything to the best of your ability.

Once you realize that there is a huge difference between criticism and feedback, you are going to be able to use feedback to feed-forward in life; use it to your advantage in all your endeavors whether personal or professional, prosper with the information and step forward towards your goals.

**"If you are not moving closer to
what you want in sales (or in life),
you probably aren't doing enough asking."**

Jack Canfield

> *Think about it ... you don't know what you don't know, so ask for feedback and listen to feedback as a way to learn and grow!*

- 49 -

YOU GIVE, YOU GET.
THE MORE YOU GIVE,
THE MORE YOU GET.
YOU DON'T GIVE, YOU DON'T GET!

**"To be able to give away riches is mandatory
if you wish to possess them.
This is the only way you will be truly rich."**

Muhammad Ali

Success in life comes quicker when you give more and stop worrying about getting more.

There are so many things in life that you simply can change. One of those things that you can change is the way that you can make people feel as well as the way that you can feel about yourself. If you think about it, there is nothing more rewarding than the feeling of being able to give to others. Whether you are handing out money to charity, buying a gift for someone who you care about or even smiling at a stranger on the sidewalk, the old saying that you get what you give rings true in many, many different ways.

You will find that there will be plenty of times in your life that you will think of only yourself. Doesn't that sound selfish? Sure. However, with the way life goes it can be easy to get caught up in material things or trying to make sure that you always come out ahead of the game. No matter what, you have to keep yourself grounded so that you do not forget that sometimes thinking of only yourself will only work against you in the end. Take the time to make yourself happy by way of giving of yourself and you are sure to feel wonderful about yourself and your life.

Focusing on the negative things in your life will end up draining you of your will to give to others. The feeling that you can receive from giving of yourself in any number of ways can help you little by little to start feeling better about yourself no matter what your current emotional, physical or financial situation may be. Start off small and begin down the path of putting others in front of you. You may be amazed at the results that will follow.

"To get joy we must give it,
to keep joy, we must scatter it."

Sir John Templeton

It all goes to the idea that when you give, you will receive tenfold. The universe has an amazing way of giving you back way more than you give. While a person may not have much to give in the way of money, they have much more love, understanding and time that they can offer. When you start helping people and giving of your time, you'll be surprised at how much others want to help and give to you.

When it comes to your business life, there are many ways that you can give of yourself here as well. Perhaps you and your company have time that you can donate to a charity in your area. Or you may find that you will want to give to a charity from your paycheck. Additionally, there may even be a co-worker that you know who has fallen on rough times. Putting together a fund between co-workers or even putting together a benefit can be amazing ways to lend a hand.

Tithing is an important aspect of life and should be done joyfully and willingly, but not feel like an obligation.

"No person was ever honored for what he received. He was honored for what he gave."

Calvin Coolidge

> ***Think about it ...*** *it's true that you get what you give. If you do not give, then you will not receive. Words to live by!*

- 50 -

HELP AND SERVE OTHERS

**"Our prime purpose in this life is to help others.
And if you can't help them,
at least don't hurt them."**

Dalai Lama

You don't have to become a personal life coach in order to help others. All it really takes is an open ear and a few words to help point people in the right direction so that they can work on all of their issues. However, in order to help others and to serve them properly, you must first work on yourself. After all, you cannot give of yourself if you do not love and believe in yourself right from the start.

Do you feel that you have something valuable that you can use to give and share with others? If so, then you can look to find ways that you can help people who surround you that are in need. Now, this need may vary from person to person to be sure. But, if you are able to give of yourself selflessly then you are going to be able to make another person stronger with your support. As challenging as it may be at times helping and serving others can be something in your life that is wonderfully rewarding. You just have to be able to give it a try.

If you hold stead fast to the belief that the more you give the more you get, then helping and serving others is one of the most important things you can do for your personal success. The best way to accomplish this is to give of yourself freely and without any expectation of receiving back, because when you genuinely care about others they will genuinely care about you.

Honesty is always the best policy, but what are you supposed to do if you feel as though the truth is going to hurt the other person. After all, you are looking to help them, not hurt them. What you need to remember is that some of the time it is necessary to hear things that are not quite as pleasant as we would like them to be in order to truly overcome the obstacles that are in our way. Whether it hurts them initially or not, they can use that information to help them on their journey.

What you may not realize is that you are already helping and serving others around you simply by being yourself. Giving great advice and setting a wonderful example are just a couple of the ways that you can be valuable to others. However, helping may be much more than a few words here and there. You may end up having to give up some of your time and creativity in order to really help out in a way that makes a difference.

If you are a person who likes to see results and change in order to feel as though they have accomplished something, then volunteer work is for you. There is nothing that is anywhere near as satisfying as helping and serving others who are in need of a helping hand. Take the time to volunteer to make care packages for our troops overseas or give up some time reading to the elderly at a local nursing home. No matter what charity you decide to focus your attention on, this time that you spend will end up being some of the most cherished and rewarding. Giving of yourself and helping and serving others comes in many forms. You simply have to find the best outlet to showcase your talents for others to be able to benefit.

"It is literally true that you can succeed best and quickest by helping others to succeed."

Napoleon Hill

Think about it ... the best way to learn is to teach, the best way to get is to give and the best way to feel good is to help and serve others!

- 51 -

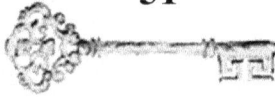

BACKWARDS PLANNING;
START WITH THE END IN MIND AND
WORK BACKWARDS

**"Our goals can only be reached
through a vehicle of a plan,
in which we must fervently believe,
and upon which we must vigorously act.
There is no other route to success."**

Stephen A. Brennan

You may have already starting planning for your life with a certain ending in mind and you didn't even realize it. If you start to think about it, this is an incredibly smart way to look to the future, by looking at the end first and then working your way backwards. Just as with any type of goal setting, you want to raise the bar to a certain level. Then you start working your way slowly toward the end goal until you achieve it or even surpass it. Because this is your destiny, then you are able to mold it any way that you would like.

If you haven't really started to look that much into the future, then you will want to start by thinking of what you would want the final picture to look like at the end. Take stock of some of the dreams that you have had in your mind and think of the things that you would like to say that you are proud of at the end. Do you have a specific person there with you that you are sharing your life with? Perhaps there is a certain career that you would like to be in or you would like to have traveled to a number of areas around the globe.

Plan your work and work your plan. Let's say you want to become a millionaire, start a new business, become the top salesperson in your company, lose some weight, maybe write a book, now you work backwards to figure out how to achieve that goal. What will you need to do to achieve different milestones along the way to reach the ultimate goal? The same holds true for all your goals whether personal and professional, plan your life and live your plan.

If you have always been the kind of person who procrastinates, then you are going to have to get out of that pattern. In order to truly plan ahead, you need to make sure that you have the drive and determination to do so. When you do not have the proper amount of drive then you are going to sit in your current lifestyle and merely grow old. Spinning your wheels in a dead end career will only keep you down and hinder your dreaming process. Nobody ever attains their goals by sitting back and watching the world pass them by.

As you move along toward your end goal, never be afraid to change it up if you feel the need to. There are many people who figure out part of the way towards their dreams that they are looking for another career or that they would even like to go for a completely different lifestyle. Simply follow your dreams and working toward your end goal moving backwards will make more sense as you go along.

**"He who would
accomplish little must sacrifice little;
he who would achieve much must sacrifice much;
he who would attain highly must sacrifice greatly."**

James Allen

Think about it ... *when you set a goal and put the plan in place with the actions needed to accomplish the goal, that's starting with the end in mind and working backwards!*

- 52 -

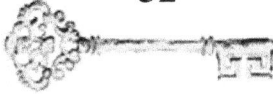

TAKE ACTION: READY, FIRE, AIM
AND ADJUST AS YOU GO

**"Create a definite plan for carrying out your desire
and begin at once, whether you ready or not,
to put this plan into action."**

Napoleon Hill

If you always do what you've done, you'll always get what you've got.

You know that you have a number of things that you must accomplish, however you are not exactly sure what your plan of attack would be. One thing is for certain, the absolute last thing you will want to do is end up procrastinating until it is too late. Sometimes you really just have to take the bull by the horns in order to get the ball rolling. Unfortunately, some of the time this may mean jumping first and thinking about the consequences later on. This is where the term 'ready, fire, aim' comes into play.

While it may not make sense to you at first, sometimes you have to just do something and then worry later on if you made the right decision or not. Half of the time, battles are fought and won on the fly. The great thing is that in life, you have the ability to try and fix your mistakes should anything go wrong. As a human being, you can make quick decisions and adjust accordingly.

"The way we get started is to quit talking and begin doing."

Walt Disney

You will learn rather quickly that you will end up becoming your own worst enemy the more that you procrastinate. Taking charge and diving in head first will allow you to get a head start on something that you may want to hold off for a long time. You have to almost think of it as quickly ripping off a band-aid. Since you know that it is going to hurt, you will find yourself babying it and pulling it off a little bit at a time. Instead, you can take action and pull it off quickly. Now you can relax and get on with something else!

In life, you must try to think way beyond what you think your limits will be. You need to know how to take chances or you will end up going through life never knowing and always wondering what could have been. You are responsible for your own actions and when it comes to your destiny, you are the only person in your driver's seat. Sure, there will be bumps in the road, but you will have to take them one by one as they come your way. You cannot go throughout your life walking on eggshells afraid of what may happen next or you are never going to go anywhere.

As an individual, you set your path. It really does not matter what order you achieve the steps along the way as long as your end results are what you have been longing for. After all, if you have three different animals standing side by side, even if you change the order that they are in you still have three different animals standing side by side.

Learning to roll with the punches is all a part of life. When you can recognize your dreams and fight for them until you are happy and successful, then you are already ahead of the game. Throughout this learning process, you will gain useful skills that you can implement to help others in your life as well.

"Action is a great restorer and builder of confidence. Inaction is not only the result, but the cause, of fear. Perhaps the action you take will be successful; perhaps different action or adjustments will have to follow. But any action is better than no action at all."

Norman Vincent Peale

> ***Think about it ...*** *nothing you do will ever be perfect; so don't wait until it is. Go for what you want or you may find yourself waiting forever to start and end up accomplishing nothing. Take action now!*

God Bless.

ABOUT THE AUTHORS

KEVIN KLIMOWSKI & JODI NICHOLSON

A FABULOUS GROUP, INC.
3837 Northdale Blvd | Suite 328
Tampa, FL 33624 | USA
T: 813.658.5026 F: 813.960.8080

ABOUT THE AUTHORS

Kevin Klimowski passed away January 2, 2011 shortly after this book was completed. He was an accomplished Speaker, Trainer and Certified Professional Success Coach. Kevin was known in the industry as a leading authority on mindset development and personal & professional growth, working with corporations and individuals on *"Improving life from the inside out."* He delivered over 1,000 presentations and trainings internationally over the past 5 years and has helped thousands of people change their lives.

His life's journey has been called a true miracle and stands as proof of the power of a positive attitude. He celebrated life daily, a survivor of leukemia, following a bone-marrow transplant eleven years ago. He and Jodi were engaged as well as successful business partners since 2000. They shared a life of true love and happiness.

Jodi Nicholson is the Founder and CEO of *A Fabulous Group, Inc.,* and *The Success Coach Institute.* She is an Author, Speaker and Master Certified Success Coach. With her entrepreneurial spirit, Jodi specializes in Business, Marketing, Motivation and Success Coaching and has been self-employed for over 25 years.

Her passion for helping others combined with her dedication to excellence is a true blessing. Whether coaching, consulting or training, Jodi consistently delivers success for her clients receiving rave reviews wherever she visits.

Her signature tagline, *"It's Okay To Be Fabulous!"* ™ really says it all! Contact Jodi at Jodi@AFabulousGroup.com

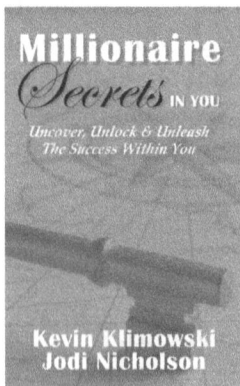

"MILLIONAIRE SECRETS IN YOU"   Book Order Form

NAME _____

ADDRESS _____

ADDRESS _____

CITY _____

STATE _____ ZIP _____

TELEPHONE _____

EMAIL _____

SEND _____ Copies @ $ _____ Each
  Plus applicable sales tax and shipping fees Add @$3.00 per book
  Actual weight varies when ordering multiple copies and cost may
  increase or decrease slightly. All orders are verified prior to ship.

TOTAL AMOUNT ENCLOSED $_____

_____
MC V DISCOVER #

EXP DATE_____ SECURITY CODE _____

_____
SIGNATURE

Mail Your Orders To: **MILLIONAIRE SECRETS IN YOU**
                       3837 NORTHDALE BLVD. SUITE 328
                       TAMPA, FL 33624

Email Orders To: **msiy@AFGOC.com**

Fax Orders To: **813-960-8080   Thank You!**

The Perfect Presentation For Your Next Event!

Millionaire Secrets in You   *Audiences Love It!*
90 Minute Inspirational Keynote, ½ Day or Full Day Training

This inspirational keynote is the perfect blend of humor and heartfelt stories wrapped around a powerful message empowering your audience to live the life of their dreams. Based on the keys from **"Millionaire Secrets in You"** we provide the disciplines your audience needs to uncover, unlock and unleash the success within them. Be sure to ask about FREE BOOKS for your audience.

Breakthrough to G.R.E.A.T.   *60 or 90 Minute*

You have everything you need inside you right now to be successful. In this high energy and experiential presentation audiences are taught the **5 Keys For A Breakthrough to G.R.E.A.T.** covering Goals, Responsibility, Education, Attitude and Team.

Build Lasting Business Relationships   *60 or 90 Minute*
Steps to Sales & Service Success That Lasts

Skill set is not as important as mindset. Learn the steps to be an excellent provider of service and successful communicator to skyrocket your sales. Build lasting business relationships that stand the test of time, earn referrals and keep your name Top of Mind with your clients and prospects. This presentation guides salespeople and executives to success as we share the secrets that continually bring attendees esteemed awards like Multi-Million Dollar Producer and Salesperson of the Year.

To arrange a speaker at your event, or to request a media kit please call 813-658-5026 or email Jodi@AFabulousGroup.com